THE SMART PERSON'S GUIDE TO ELDERCARE

By Jodi Lyons

W9-AlO-435

Keith Publications, LLC
www.keithpublications.com
©2013

Arizona
USA

THE SMART PERSON'S GUIDE TO ELDERCARE

Copyright© 2013

By Jodi Lyons

Edited Kat Daoud
www.kjdaoud.com

Cover art by Elisa Elaine Luevanos
www.ladymaverick81.com

Cover art Keith Publications, LLC © 2013
www.keithpublications.com

ISBN: 978-1-936372-70-6

If you are interested in purchasing more works of this nature, please stop by
www.keithpublications.com

Contact information: info@keithpublications.com
Visit us at: www.keithpublications.com

Printed in The United States of America

Dedication

To my mother, father and sister with thanks
and gratitude for their love and support.

Acknowledgements

I am grateful to my agent, Diane Nine,
for her wise counsel and continual support.
I thank my editor, Katrina Daoud,
for her patience and attention to detail.
Words alone are not enough to thank my clients,
friends and colleagues who encouraged me to write this book
and kept me supplied with caffeine while I did.
I couldn't have done this without them.
Last, but certainly not least, to my mother Linda Lyons,
my father Ed Lyons and
my sister Shari Lyons -- thank you for everything!
I love you.

Introduction

Why did I write this book? The eldercare system in the United States has become such a tangled spider web that it's virtually impossible to navigate.

While I was the Chief Executive Officer of an international long-term care association, I saw first-hand the complexity of the system and the incredible disparity in the types of care available in different regions. As an eldercare consultant tasked with matching clients to appropriate care, I saw the human toll navigating the system takes from those seeking help. As a board member of the Alzheimer's Association, National Capital Area, I saw the real life, practical effects of healthcare policy decisions and funding disparities.

To be honest, what I saw scared me. My primary concern was, with such disparity in services offered, quality of care and regulation/supervision, there was no way for an individual consumer to make an educated decision about his or her eldercare needs without extending an extraordinary amount of time, energy and money. How is the average consumer supposed to know the difference between the best providers and the worst?

Most consultants limit their service area. Therefore, they cannot compare their local care providers to the best providers. They can give you the best of the region, but if the region in general has lousy providers, you are stuck picking the "least worst", not the best.

In my opinion, this is NOT the way to choose care.

My second concern was the plethora of bad information available. Different marketing people from different care providers use the same words to mean different things. Each type of eldercare is regulated differently—some are not regulated on a national level at all—and each state has different exemptions. Quite frankly, even the national regulations and inspections do not tell the whole story. So, truly evaluating the quality of care is a nightmare.

My third concern was that people did not really know what type of care they needed. Searching the Internet without this knowledge is nothing more than flipping through an electronic phonebook and hoping you find the right provider.

This is where my book comes in.

My goal is to create educated consumers. I want older adults and their families to clearly understand how to determine their specific needs and find the best care available for them. I want them to know what questions to ask, what answers to expect and what the answers mean.

Table of Contents

Chapter 1

Defining the Issues

First things first. How to determine if there is there a problem.

A. How do you know when your family member needs help?

The simple answer is there is no easy answer. It depends on your family member. In some families, you may not know until something drastic happens. For example, your mother may fall in the bathroom and no one finds her for a day or so. Only after that happens will she admit to you she has been dizzy and feeling weak for a few months or has fallen before.

On the other hand, you may have a family member who complains about everything. In that case, it becomes very difficult to find out what the real problem is. The challenge here is determining whether the physical aches and pains are caused or exacerbated by depression or loneliness.

The best advice I can offer is—ASK! Be blunt. Sometimes we have to discuss things that are uncomfortable, overly personal, even borderline inappropriate. However, addressing the potential issues before they become crises is very important.

Keep in mind at all times, the person you are talking with is an adult, not a child. One of the greatest fears older adults have is losing control of their choices. Some do not want to become burdens on their families while others feel they are entitled to be cared for in a manner THEY deem appropriate. So, be honest when you discuss the things that worry you and be sure to involve the senior as much as possible in any decision-making.

Finally, while I am a big advocate of seniors' rights, I also recognize that safety is a major concern. If something truly is unsafe, you may need to take action without first obtaining a family consensus.

"I can't believe my mother..." Situations that raise concern
Stories from adult children who thought their parents might need

The spoiled milk:

My friend went to visit her father and found three gallon containers of milk on the counter and none in the 'fridge. Perhaps needless to say, they were quite rancid. She thought it odd when she had spoken to her father three times that week and each time he was walking to the store to get milk, but didn't really question it. Unfortunately, he had a brain tumor and it was beginning to affect his ability to function. He knew he needed milk, and he knew where to get it, but he couldn't remember to put it in the 'fridge.

The million dollar driveway:

A woman went to visit her ninety-four year old father and noticed his driveway was newly sealed. He proudly told her that some men had come by the house and offered to do the driveway for ten thousand dollars but he had negotiated with them and only paid six thousand. The catch? The driveway was only two car lengths long and one car width wide. It probably was a five hundred dollar job and a common scam, AND— he paid by check so the crooks now had his bank account info and signature. Fortunately, he lived in an area where the police department was on top of things. They got some of his money back and told the family how to work with the bank to prevent any additional fraud.

The road trip to nowhere:

An older adult in a rural area decided to go for a drive to visit some family members. He got in his car for the hour drive and headed off down the road. Four hours later, he still had not arrived. The police found him when he stopped at a gas station three states away to fill his tank. He had no idea where he was or where he was going. He just kept driving straight until he needed gas.

The broken hip:

This story is all too common…Mom falls in the bathroom, breaks her hip and can't reach the phone that's on the counter. She can't crawl or move and stays on the floor until someone gets worried when they can't reach her. She might even be wearing the emergency response pendant but doesn't remember to push it. By the time anyone finds her, she's weak, dehydrated and therefore has to be hospitalized and then sent to a nursing home for rehabilitation.

The accountant saw it first:

Mom seemed fine and was perfectly able to handle her own business affairs and maintain her house with a little help from a cleaning service. At least, that's what the family thought before the accountant noticed a one hundred-thousand dollar withdrawal from the investment account! Turns out Mom had been visited by a nice young man who was going door-to-door selling annuities. So, she bought one. Too bad it was a fraud.

The common thread of the above stories is there was a triggering event—a big wakeup call for the family that things were not as good as they seemed and that the older adults needed help.

Below are some less obvious triggers.

"Looking back, I realize this should have worried me…"
Situations that SHOULD raise concern and often do not

The story of the overworked washing machine:

One of my friends called me to ask if I thought it was strange that his parents always had a load of laundry running when he visited. My own mother always does tons of laundry, so I probably wouldn't have had the same concern, but this was unusual for his family. It turns out he visited three times a week and while the laundry was running, the hamper still had dirty clothes in it, the dishtowels were dirty and the towels in the bathroom smelled like ammonia. When he asked his parents about why they were doing so much laundry, they got very defensive and started yelling at him that he should worry about his own laundry, buy a bigger house, go on a diet, get married—anything to change the subject. This situation should raise questions about incontinence and/or mobility issues in getting to the bathroom.

The story of the unlabeled cans:

I remember as a child going to visit my grandparents in Florida. I always was mesmerized by the closet full of sugar free gelatin (hundreds of boxes).The things that truly fascinated me, however, were the shelves filled with unlabeled soup cans. At least, we think they were soup. It turns out a major soup manufacturer had some kind of free prize if you turned in your labels. So, my grandparents dutifully peeled off all of the labels and mailed them in. Dinner for the next few months always was a surprise—we never knew what was in the can we were opening—could be soup, could be vegetables. As I look back, I am glad we questioned this behavior. While it ended up being funny, it could have been a sign of problems still to come. It could have been that they went to the supermarket and forgot they had already bought twelve cans of soup and twelve boxes of gelatin—an early warning sign of dementia. It also could have been a sign they were worried about money and therefore were hoarding food (not uncommon in people who lived through the Great Depression).

The story of the unpolished fingernails:

I have a friend who ALWAYS has her nails done. Until recently, no one ever saw her with a single chip in her nail polish. Recently though, her nails are chipped, broken and look horrible. She's also self-conscious about it, so she has been acting differently. She has been working two jobs and taking care of ill family members out of town and therefore hasn't had time to care for herself. Changes in personal grooming habits are a neon sign warning of impending trouble. A caregiver who exhibits these changes is stretched too thin and needs help. A senior citizen who exhibits these changes may be unable to bathe easily, drive to the beauty salon, or may be exhibiting signs of depression or early stages of dementia. In either case, the situation needs to be addressed.

Conclusion:

You should be concerned when: Something seems unusual, out of place, or wrong.
Behaviors change and it seems like more than just a bad day.

"I knew I had a crisis when..."
Stories from adult children who realized their parents were in severe trouble even though they thought things were under control

But, Dad was the sick one:

It's the scenario most older adults are afraid of...The well spouse dies before the sick one. You know the story—your friend's parents live in the home they raised their kids in, Mom is taking care of Dad who has dementia. The family thinks she has everything under control until she dies and Dad doesn't understand how to call for help. I've heard many stories of the person with dementia not pushing the emergency response button when the spouse needs help because the button is for when the person wearing it needs help, The unexpected death of the caregiver causes an immediate care crisis, usually exacerbated by lack of financial and legal preparation for this scenario—causing a logistical nightmare for a family that's already in mourning.

But, she had a monitoring system:

One of my friends got worried when she hadn't heard from her dad for a few days, but she assumed one of her many sisters had brought their dad to their home—a regular occurrence. Their dad had an emergency response system and my friend had not been contacted by the company, so it was easy to assume everything was ok. It wasn't. It turned out Dad had gotten so weak and dehydrated he was unable to get out of bed, and was so confused he did not know how to push the emergency response pendant he was wearing. As best as we can guess, he'd been lying in bed, unable to get up, for more than twenty-four hours.

But, she only drives to church:

This is one of my scariest wake-up calls because it has the potential to hurt or kill innocent people...I can't tell you how many times dangerous drivers are allowed to continue to drive because no one reports them. Their families hesitate to take away the car and their family member's independence, and often hide behind the excuses of "she only drives to church every morning", "he only drives to the grocery store three miles away" or "she doesn't drive at night". I say the destination doesn't matter. The fact that the driver can't see well, hear well, react quickly enough, or has cognitive impairment (or all of the above) should be enough reason to take the car away. Yet, people most often won't do so until there's an accident. The gentlest accident was when a client's mom hit four PARKED cars in the parking lot of her apartment complex— and kept on driving!

B. Is this really a crisis?

Learning the difference between a true crisis, a short-term problem and a long-term problem

1. Is this a dire emergency?

Warning signs that require immediate medical attention.

First things first. If you think this may possibly be a medical emergency, dial 911 and let a trained medical professional make a judgment. That is what they are there for. Do not be embarrassed if it turns out to be something less than a dire emergency. You are NOT bothering the police department, fire department, ambulance crew, and etcetera.

If your family member calls you complaining of anything you think could be an emergency, stay on the line with them and call their emergency services number from your cell phone or another line in your house.

HELPFUL HINT:

Program the direct dial emergency number for the fire department, police department and/or ambulance dispatcher that serves your family member into your cell phone and keep a copy elsewhere. Remember 911 goes to YOUR dispatcher and your call will have to be relayed—you want to make sure the emergency dispatcher closest to your family member gets called as quickly as possible.

Below are some warning signs that require immediate medical attention:

<u>Warning signs of stroke:</u>

Sudden numbness or weakness of the face, arm or leg, especially on one side of the body

Sudden confusion, trouble speaking or understanding

Sudden trouble seeing in one or both eyes

Sudden trouble walking, dizziness, loss of balance or coordination

Sudden, severe headache with no known cause [1]

For more information on strokes, please visit the American Stroke Association, a division of the American Heart Association, at www.strokeassociation.org.

Warning signs of heart attack:
Chest discomfort. Most heart attacks involve discomfort in the center of the chest that lasts more than a few minutes, or goes away and comes back. It can feel like uncomfortable pressure, squeezing, fullness or pain.

Discomfort in other areas of the upper body. Symptoms can include pain or discomfort in one or both arms, the back, neck, jaw or stomach.

Shortness of breath. This feeling often comes along with chest discomfort. Be aware that it can occur before the chest discomfort. Other signs: These may include breaking out in a cold sweat, nausea or lightheadedness[2]

Also, please be aware women sometimes exhibit different signs than those listed above. When in doubt, call 911.

For more information on heart attacks, please visit the Act in Time website—a joint project between the American Heart Association and National Heart, Lung and Blood Institute of the National Institutes of Health. http://www.nhlbi.nih.gov/actintime/

2. Is this a big problem that needs a solution in a day or two?

So, you've determined there is a problem and it is not a dire emergency. The next step is to determine how soon this problem needs to be addressed. Remember, we have just eliminated this situation as being a crisis since it did not involve dialing 911.

First, take a deep breath. If you find yourself thinking this situation needs to be resolved in a day or two, then most likely, your family member is in the hospital. If not, you probably have had a scare, but realistically have a few days to find a solution.

Let us start with the hospital part first. When your family member is getting ready to be discharged from the hospital, s/he should have been visited by a social worker or a nurse who has developed a discharge plan if further care is needed. Meaning, if your family member cannot return home and take care of him/herself SAFELY, someone in the hospital needs to address this situation.

Speak to the hospital's social service department and your family member's physician. This is not the time to be shy. Ask the social workers, nurses, doctors <u>and the patient</u> if your family member will be able to shop for food, prepare food, eat, bathe, clothe him/herself, get and take medication and get to and from the toilet safely. If you have any questions about his/her ability to do so, do not stop nagging the social services department and the doctor until you have a list of what needs to be done and who will do it.

The discharge planners should be able to help you to find a home health aide, rehabilitation facility, nursing home, and etcetera. You may be forced to choose one of the recommended service providers very quickly. While I know this is NOT the ultimate way to choose the care provider, it may be unavoidable. You certainly can ask to increase the hospital stay for a few days, but not indefinitely. You also are walking the fine line between wanting to leave the hospital and finding a facility that has an available bed.

Also remember your family member is not required to stay forever in the facility you choose at this point. So, while you need to do your due diligence and check out the service provider, do not panic. It is entirely possible to find a fine short-term rehabilitation center to meet your immediate needs even if it is not someplace you would like your family member to live for an extended period. It also is possible to have your family member move home and have a home health aide for a short time as you explore other options. This is, however, a great way to get your family member into a nursing home that is a good long term option—there often is more flexibility in available beds if you enter via short-term rehabilitation. So, do not hesitate to "shoot for the stars" and approach the best (or your first choice) nursing home or rehabilitation facility.

Above all, remember you need to deal with the specific, immediate need. You are not expected to, nor may it be possible to, solve all of the immediate and future needs, explore every possible option and make a final unchangeable decision at this particular moment.

If your family member is on Medicare or Medicaid, remember there are very specific rules the care providers must follow. Make sure you clearly understand what is covered and what is not. For example, you may hear Medicare will cover X number of nurse visits per week. How many hours does that cover? What exactly will the nurse do? What other services does your parent need? Who will provide those services? Who will pay for those services?

HELPFUL HINT: WATCH OUT FOR SHARKS AND VULTURES.

There are many incredibly good attorneys and financial planners who would be helpful in this situation, and there are many who are not. Please, please, please—stop, listen and think before you make a legal and financial plan. There are some immediate needs, like powers of attorney, do not resuscitate orders, and advanced directives—and you should address these as soon as possible. Remember, Medicaid has a multi-year look back. Make sure you and your attorney/financial planner take the look-back window into account before you make a plan. There are many disreputable professionals who will tell you they will save your loved ones assets from the government or Medicaid, etcetera. You need to make sure you clearly understand what money is needed to pay for the care your loved one needs, what Medicare and Medicaid pay for and that any plan you make is compliant with the look-back window.

What if there was no hospital stay, but it still seems like a crisis?

Let us say your family member is making you nervous. She or he is not eating well, the house is a mess, the laundry is piled up to the ceiling, the trash is overflowing, there is rotten food in the refrigerator and you suspect she or he is not taking medication appropriately. This is a problem to be sure, but it is NOT a crisis. It can be fixed, and you have a day or two to take care of it.

First, ask your family member if s/he is having difficulty with specific things. Use the geriatric assessment tool later in this book. It is important to clearly define the problem(s) and not to generalize. This is NOT the time to say "the house is too big for you to keep up and you have to move". It may be a very simple problem – maybe the washer and dryer are too far away when they are carrying laundry. Maybe the trash cans are too heavy to lift or your family member cannot bend down well enough to empty the small cans. These are things that can be solved easily with a wheeled laundry cart or putting the little garbage can on a small stool to raise it off the floor.

Second, determine what kind of help is needed. Housekeeping? Medication assistance? Meal preparation?

For the immediate needs, I would call a home health agency to provide as many services as possible. Remember to find one that is licensed, bonded, insured and conducts national background checks. Then you can look for longer term solutions.

3. Is there time to plan a long-term solution?

So, you have survived the crisis and the big scare. Or, you have been lucky and managed to avoid it. Now is the time to do some long-term planning. First and foremost, understand there is no one solution—there are many. Only you and your family can best determine what fits your needs.

There are some common misconceptions I would like to address before we go any further.

Staying at home:
First, while many people would like to stay in their own homes, many do not. While staying at home is familiar, it often can be lonely—especially if one spouse has died. So, do not assume your family member wants to stay at home—ask. I was very surprised when some very spry eighty-five year-olds came to my office

wanting to sell their house and move to a retirement community or assisted living. They wanted to be somewhere where they could have assistance if needed, and just as importantly, they wanted to be somewhere they could step outside and join a friend for a cup of tea, play a game of bridge or just sit and chat. They no longer wanted to have to drive everywhere.

<u>Nursing homes:</u>
As soon as people hear these words, they conjure up pictures of dark, smelly institutions with long, dirty, linoleum-covered hallway lined with sick people in hospital gowns sitting in their wheelchairs along the corridor. Unfortunately, some places were like that. NOW, MOST ARE NOT!

Where do we begin? First, nursing home refers to a specific type of care provider. Healthy people do not move into nursing homes, so yes, you will see old, frail and sick people there. Some may be in wheelchairs, some will be in special beds, some will be incontinent and some will have fully developed dementia. The residents of a nursing home need skilled care—care that cannot normally be provided by an untrained person.

Today's good nursing homes are clean, bright, cheery and provide good social activities and mental stimulation in addition to advanced medical care. Many are part of a campus that also contains independent living and assisted living. Many provide specialized Alzheimer's/dementia care.

Remember you are dealing with many choices of care options, not just nursing homes, and the nursing homes you are choosing among are NOT the ones your family member is afraid of. While some really bad ones still do exist, you can and should choose not to go there.

Again, I repeat. Healthy people do NOT move into nursing homes. So, when you broach the subject of moving with your family member, understand they may be picturing the old-style nursing home their elderly relatives died in many years ago. It is important you reassure your family member this is NOT what you are talking about.

Assisted Living:

First and foremost, it is vital to understand the services offered by Assisted Living vary widely among providers. Second, Medicaid does NOT usually pay for assisted living (there may be some exceptions through state waiver programs).Third, it is important to understand the fee structure of the particular provider you are considering. Most assisted living providers quite reasonably charge more for more complicated care. Make sure you have done your math correctly.

Independent Living/Retirement Communities:

As in assisted living above, retirement communities normally are private-pay and vary widely in the care/services provided. Know what you are buying and know what you can afford.

Other options:

There are many other types of care options. The most important advice is to be an educated consumer— make sure the care is good, appropriate for today's needs and flexible enough to take care of tomorrow's needs. Remember—no care is free.

4. Is this a problem we predict will happen down the road?

Planning in advance is wonderful! Just remember no one can predict the future entirely, so the best we can do is pick a few types of care and a few care providers in each category, hoping we have covered our bases.

First, pick the geographic region(s) you want to explore. You would be surprised how often family members are excited about moving nearer to their children, grandchildren or good friends.

Second, get the financial house in order. I STRONGLY recommend having your family member sit down with his/her attorney, accountant and financial planner NOW. All at once. Many of these professionals will sit down with each other and you for an hour or so without charging you. Why all at once? You want to make sure all are on the same page—making sure your family member will get the care s/he needs in a place that will make him/her happy. Many of us are living longer than we expected, so it is vital to make sure we have the ability to pay for our care. Yes, there are programs to assist elderly in paying for care— Medicare and Medicaid being the two most well-known—but being entirely dependent on these severely limits your choices of types of care provided and the care providers themselves.

So, that explains the accountant and the financial planner. Why is the attorney there? To make sure all legal documents are in order—wills, powers of attorney, living wills or other relevant documents. Basically, all the things you will need if your family member becomes incapacitated.

While all three are meeting, be sure you and your family member understand exactly who among these people will be responsible for each task. You want to be sure they work as a team to protect your family member's interests and assets.

Defining the areas where help is needed

Preliminary geriatric assessment questions
The first question most people should ask is: Does your loved one require care? The second is if he or she does, how much care is needed?

C. Family Needs Assessment

Does your loved one require care? If so, how much care is needed?

The checklist below is designed to help you to answer these questions.

For each question below, place a check mark next to the description that best fits your family member or friend.

There are some important things to keep in mind while you review this checklist.

1. Be kind and honest with your family member or friend. This checklist is a guide, not a diagnosis. The person in need of care and other family members may think you are overstepping your bounds, jumping to conclusions or otherwise becoming involved in a situation in which you have no right.

2.   Having said the above, odds are something triggered your decision to evaluate your family member's health and safety. Trust your instincts. The checklist may show your family member is fine, or help you determine specific areas where your family member needs help. Be realistic and honest in your assessment. For example, is the older adult really able to dress himself if it takes him ninety minutes every morning and ninety minutes every night to do so?

3.   Repeat this checklist every few months so you can track any improvement or decline. Do not forget to note the date and time you complete the checklist.

4.   Remember the purpose of finding care for your family member is to provide them with a safe and healthy environment in which they have the most independence and dignity possible. Emphasis here on SAFE, There is a movement in the eldercare industry towards least restrictive environment—meaning, keep people in their homes as long as possible. However, I would argue (and have!) if the person is lonely and unsafe, moving into a community/care provider often is the preferred option. Home is not always better than a residential care provider.

5.   Also be honest about the time and resources available to help the family member or friend. o not underestimate the effort required to be a caregiver. It is okay to use professional help and in some cases, necessary and preferable.

6.   Do not forget the cup of coffee factor. Many people prefer to stay at home, but it is also vitally important not to create a shut-in who has no human interaction for days at a time. The question we ask is:"If you want to have a cup of coffee (or tea) with someone, what do you have to do to make it happen?"If the answer is that it is impossible or requires a big effort, staying at home may not be the best option. There are many types of choices, not just staying at home or going to a nursing home, and at this point in the process, it is best to keep options open.

7.   This checklist is no substitute for medical advice or medical care. It is a starting place for your discussions with the appropriate

medical personnel.
Checklist

Remember, no one is perfect. Look for patterns and give your family member the benefit of the doubt. The goal is to ensure safety, health and well-being while preserving as much independence as possible.

The questions are loosely organized into three categories: personal, around the house and interacting with the outside world. Of course, there is a lot of overlap, but we have found grouping the questions helps family members think about where and when the senior needs help.

Personal:

1. Communication

A.   No difficulty reading, writing or comprehending.

B.   Occasional trouble recalling words. Reads less. Sometimes asks for information to be repeated, then comprehends. Handwriting may be less legible than before.

C.   Frequent trouble recalling words. Avoids reading. Frequently asks for information to be repeated yet still may not comprehend. Handwriting deteriorates.

D.   Significant problems with reading, writing, comprehension. Difficulty maintaining a conversation.

2. Judgment/Mental Function

A.   Exercises good judgment. Makes appropriate decisions. No trouble recalling people, places, appointments.

B.   Exercises reasonably good judgment but requires some help or prompting. Experiences occasional memory lapses.

C.   Does not exercise good judgment. Frequently needs help making decisions; often appears confused. Shows significant memory lapses.

D.   Judgment and memory are significantly unreliable. Needs considerable help making decisions.

3. Mood

Before you answer this question, please think about the following: As a family member/caregiver, do you receive phone calls expressing anger, depression, or in crisis-mode when it seems like it is not really a crisis? Do you feel you are expected to jump through hoops or drop everything you are doing or the person will fall apart emotionally? Recognizing these often are signs of a senior's loneliness or depression, let us address the senior's mood:

A.   Reasonably good morale and self-esteem. Usually copes well with everyday stress, grieves loss then carries on with life.

B.   Displays occasional anxiety, depression, irritability or fear that sometimes interferes with normal functioning.

C.   Displays anxiety, depression, irritability or fear that often interferes with normal functioning.

D.   Mood problems are prevalent. The person may become unmanageable or you fear s/he will cause harm to him/herself or others.

4. Medications

Also think about how the person GETS his/her medicine. Does the pharmacy deliver? Can they get to the pharmacy by themselves?

A.   Takes own medication as directed with few lapses.

B.   Sometimes confused about which medications to take. Occasionally takes the wrong ones.

C.   Needs regular supervision to take medications.

D.   Depends on others to manage medication.

5. Alcohol or Substance Abuse (includes abuse of prescription medication)

A.   No problem.

B.   Empty liquor bottles or medicine bottles appear in the garbage or throughout the home with disturbing frequency but the person seems unimpaired.

C.   Signs of substance abuse increase. The person appears impaired.

D.   Person exhibits disruptive behavior.

6. Personal Safety

A.   Is conscious of safety. Remembers to turn off the stove, lock the doors, wear a seatbelt, etcetera.

B.   Occasional safety lapses.

C.   Frequent safety lapses.

D.   Lacks awareness of safety issues, posing a potential threat to him or herself or others.

7. Toileting

A.   Needs no help.

B.   Needs some help—occasional accidents.

C.   Needs more help—frequent incidents of wetting or soiling.

D.   Cannot toilet alone.

8. Bathing

A.   Bathes regularly and thoroughly without assistance.

B.   Needs help getting into or out of the tub or shower.

C.   Needs regular assistance with bathing—may try to avoid it.

D.   Seems unconcerned about personal cleanliness. Cannot bathe satisfactorily even with considerable help.

9. Grooming

A.   Grooms satisfactorily without assistance.

B.   Occasionally may neglect to comb hair, may have trouble brushing teeth or shaving.

C.   Needs considerable help with grooming.

D.   Seems unconcerned about appearance. Cannot groom without assistance.

10. Dressing

A.   Dresses appropriately without help.

B.   May have difficulty with buttons, jewelry or ties. May need help choosing clothes.

C.   Relies on someone else to choose clothes and help with dressing.

D.   Needs help with nearly all aspects of dressing.

Around The House:

11. Meals

Take into consideration the following: Is this a case of cannot prepare a meal (even using the microwave), does not like to cook, cannot shop, or does not like to eat alone? Also, think about whether the person has lost interest in food or if they still eat with enjoyment if you take them out to a restaurant.

A.   Prepares appropriate meals. Eats without assistance.

B.   Occasionally has difficulty preparing meals. Sometimes lets refrigerator or pantry become bare or allows food to spoil. Eats without assistance.

C.   Needs some help preparing meals or eating. Cannot maintain refrigerator or pantry without assistance. Frequently allows food to spoil.

D.   Unable to prepare meals. Cannot eat without assistance.

12. Grocery Shopping

A.   Purchases groceries without assistance.

B.   May forget items resulting in more frequent trips to the supermarket. Pantry is not well stocked.

C.   Pantry is in a state of disarray. Needs help to shop. Seems more forgetful and intimidated or confused by the supermarket.

D.   Unable to shop even with assistance.

13. Finances

A.   Needs no help with banking, paying bills or balancing the checkbook.

B.   Easily makes routine purchases but may have difficulty paying bills or balancing the checkbook.

C.   Needs help to manage finances.

D.   Cannot manage finances.

14. Housekeeping

A.   Maintains a home at appropriate levels of cleanliness and neatness.

B.   Can perform most housekeeping tasks with a few lapses in neatness (may allow newspapers to pile up).

C.   Needs help to maintain a home at appropriate levels of neatness and cleanliness.

D.   Unable to maintain a home. Seems unconcerned about neatness and cleanliness or overwhelmed by the inability to maintain a home.

15. Laundry

A.   Takes care of clothing and does laundry without assistance.

B.   Has some difficulty identifying special care items such as dry cleaning or hand-washing.

C.   Needs help to do laundry.

D.   Relies on someone else to do laundry.

Interacting with the outside world:

16. Behavior

If you are out in public with this person, are you embarrassed by his/her behavior? Do you avoid public social situations with the senior?

A.   Usually acts appropriately in social situations.

B.   Occasionally acts in an unusual way, for example, wearing the same shirt every day. Finds unreasonable fault with others.

C.   Disturbing behavior. You may find yourself avoiding social situations with this person because his/her behavior draws the attention of others.

D.   The person no longer can function socially.

17. Mobility

Does the person decline social invitations because of mobility issues? If the person remains at home, have we created a shut-in?

Walks satisfactorily for his/her age. Needs no help with stairs, escalators or revolving doors.

A.   Slow when walking. Sometimes needs help with stairs, escalators or revolving doors.

B.   Avoids walking. Often needs assistance – may use a cane or walker.

C.   Cannot walk unassisted. Climbing stairs is difficult or impossible.

18. Social Life (this includes the cup of coffee factor mentioned earlier)

A.   Maintains usual level of interpersonal relationships.

B.   Occasionally has difficulty with interpersonal relationships.

C.   Needs assistance and or prompting to maintain relationships.

D.   Not interested in or concerned about others.

19. Driving or Other Transportation

A.   Drives or arranges for other transportation.

B.   Sometimes ignores stop signs or traffic lights. May have been involved in minor accidents. May not drive at the appropriate speed. Sometimes struggles to arrange other transportation (for example, calling a taxi).

C.   Makes passengers feel unsafe. Sometimes struggles to arrange other transportation (for example, calling a taxi).

D.   No longer able to drive safely. Usually needs help to arrange other transportation.

20. Telephone
A.   Converses appropriately, can look up phone numbers, manage a cordless phone or cell phone.

B.   Sometimes seems distracted or confused during phone conversations. Sometimes misplaces the cordless phone or cell phone.

C.   Frequently seems distracted or confused during phone conversations. Often misplaces the cordless phone or forgets to hang up the phone.

D.   Has significant trouble using the phone and may avoid using it.

What do the scores mean?

An "A" response means your family member is fine in this area. A

"B" response means assistance might be necessary.

A "C" response means assistance is needed. The next step will be to determine the best way to receive that help – either through home care or in a residential facility.

A "D" response in more than one or two categories means this person needs full-time assistance – either through home care or in a residential facility.

Now Onto Questions That Are as Important as the Twenty Listed Above.

1. Do you (or your siblings/spouse/kids) feel overwhelmed, torn or pressured about your caregiving responsibilities?

A.   never

B.   sometimes

C.   often

D.   frequently

2. Do your caregiving responsibilities interfere with your job, childcare responsibilities, household responsibilities or

relationships?

A.   never

B.   sometimes

C.   often

D.   frequently

3. Do your caregiving responsibilities affect your health (physical and emotional)?

A.   never

B.   sometimes

C.   often

D.   frequently

C. What Else Do You Need to Consider?

Is this Alzheimer's disease, dementia or forgetfulness?

Alzheimer's disease (pronounced *AHLZ-hi-merz*) is a complex disease that affects the brain. Approximately 4.5 million Americans have this disease. Although many things about Alzheimer's remain a mystery, research continues to bring us a better understanding of the disease, more accurate diagnoses and more effective treatments.

Alzheimer's disease is one of several disorders that cause the gradual loss of brain cells. The disease was first described in 1906 by German physician Dr. Alois Alzheimer. Although the disease was once considered rare, research has shown it is the leading cause of dementia.[3]

What is the difference between Alzheimer's and dementia? Dementia is a generic term for many symptoms that signify a decline in thinking skills. Some of these symptoms include personality changes, gradual loss of memory, impaired judgment, behavioral problems and a decreasing ability to perform routine tasks.

Alzheimer's disease is a specific type of dementia. The onset and progression of Alzheimer's varies incredibly from person to person. The disease may last for a few years or as many as twenty years. Also, symptoms can range from mild cognitive impairment to complete loss of function.

If you are worried about a family member, it does not really matter whether you use the words dementia or Alzheimer's—only a trained physician is going to be able to make a specific diagnosis. However, you should look at the results of the checklist you completed earlier and compare it to the Alzheimer's Association's warning signs below.

Keep in mind some change in memory is normal as we grow older. The symptoms of Alzheimer's disease are more than simple lapses in memory, however. People with Alzheimer's or related dementias experience difficulties communicating, learning, thinking and reasoning—problems <u>severe enough to have an impact on an individual's work, social activities and family life.</u>[4]

The Alzheimer's Association believes it is critical for people with dementia and their families to receive information, care and support as early as possible. To help family members and health care professionals recognize warning signs of Alzheimer's disease, the association has developed a checklist of common symptoms.

Memory loss. One of the most common early signs of dementia is forgetting recently learned information. While it is normal to forget appointments, names or telephone numbers, those with dementia will forget such things more often and not remember them later.

Difficulty performing familiar tasks. People with dementia often find it hard to complete everyday tasks that are so familiar we usually do not think about how to do them. A person with Alzheimer's may not know the steps for preparing a meal, using a household appliance or participating in a lifelong hobby.

Problems with language. Everyone has trouble finding the right word sometimes, but a person with Alzheimer's disease often forgets simple words or substitutes unusual words, making his or her speech or writing hard to understand. If a person with Alzheimer's is unable to find his or her toothbrush, for example, the individual may ask for "that thing for my mouth."

Disorientation to time and place. It is normal to forget the day of the week or where you are going. People with Alzheimer's disease can become lost on their own street, forget where they are and how they got there and not know how to get back home.

Poor or decreased judgment. No one has perfect judgment all the time. Those with Alzheimer's may dress without regard to the weather, wearing several shirts or blouses on a warm day or very little clothing in cold weather. Individuals with dementia often show poor judgment about money, giving away large amounts of money to telemarketers or paying for home repairs or products they do not need.

Problems with abstract thinking. Balancing a checkbook may be hard when the task is more complicated than usual. Someone with Alzheimer's disease could forget completely what the numbers are and what needs to be done with them.

Misplacing things. Anyone can temporarily misplace a wallet or key. A person with Alzheimer's disease may put things in unusual places: an iron in the freezer or a wristwatch in the sugar bowl.

Changes in mood or behavior. Everyone can become sad or moody from time to time. Someone with Alzheimer's disease can show rapid mood swings—from calm to tears to anger—for no apparent reason.

Changes in personality. People's personalities ordinarily change somewhat with age, but a person with Alzheimer's disease can change a lot, becoming extremely confused, suspicious, fearful or dependent on a family member.

Loss of initiative. It is normal to tire of housework, business activities or social obligations at times. The person with Alzheimer's disease may become very passive, sitting in front of the television for hours, sleeping more than usual or not wanting to do usual activities.[5]

1. Where to go if you need more help at this stage.

Depending on the responses to the above questions, you probably are feeling overwhelmed right now. If you are concerned about the results of the checklist or the Alzheimer's list, now would be a good time to meet with your family member's physician. Then, if s/he is not board certified in geriatrics, I would ask for a referral to someone who is. Another option is to call a geriatric social worker who can conduct a complete geriatric assessment and hook you up with some support networks. I would still talk to the doctor, but meeting with the social worker first may help you to prepare for your conversation.

Then, you may be referred to a neurologist or neuropsychologist for further testing. One important factor – regardless of the age of the person you are worried about – be assertive, even pushy, if you think you are not being taken seriously. Young people can get dementia, too. Young onset (often called early onset) Alzheimer's is real, and often misdiagnosed. Front temporal dementia (often called FTD or Pick's disease) is real, and often affects younger people.

The Alzheimer's Association is a wealth of information for patients, their families and physicians. You can contact them at:
Alzheimer's Association, www.alz.org, 800.272.3900

National office
225 North Michigan Avenue Floor 17
Chicago, IL 60601-7633
Telephone: 800.272.3900
Telephone: 312.335.8700
Fax: 312.335.1110

Or, check their website at www.alz.org to find a chapter near you. I especially appreciate that this organization has people available twenty-four hours a day for information, referrals or support:

Twenty-four-hour Contact Center Telephone: 800.272.3900
E-mail:info@alz.org

D. What family resources realistically are available.
1. How to determine availability of time, expertise, money.
Remember, no guilt. You may want to have your family member move in with you, or you may not. You may want to provide full-time care for your family member or you may not. The important thing is to take care of your family member, yourself and other family members. It does no one any good to take on more than you realistically can or want to handle. There is no shame in this. It simply is true. Most importantly, there are professionals out there who can provide excellent care. The best thing to do is to make a chart of what is needed to care for your family member. Include everything from the twenty questions you asked above. If money is an issue, estimate how much is needed and put that on the list too. Send this list to everyone involved. Then, sit down with all family members who are involved— or set up a conference call—and go item by item to see what individual family members can and are willing to do. Remember, their choosing to do anything at all is voluntary.

2. Questions to ask family members and common misconceptions to avoid.

First, do not assume. Just because someone is not married or does not have kids does not mean they have more free time than someone who does. They may have a very demanding job or something else that keeps them busy. Conversely, do not assume a stay-at-home mother has nothing but free time, or is too busy with the kids to do anything else. Also, many families make the mistake of assuming male family members are incompetent, so they rely on wives, daughters-in-law, nieces, and etcetera. Do not forget the sons, sons-in-law and nephews. Older grandchildren can be great caregivers too.

Second, be honest. If your family member cannot get to the bathroom alone, you really need someone to be there all the time— even at night. This is a lot for a family to handle by themselves. It is especially difficult on a spouse who may be elderly him/herself.

Third, do not forget to ask the one who needs care what s/he wants. You may have to really press to get an answer. Meaning, you may have to ask many times and be very specific. No one wants to be a burden and no one wants to lose their independence. If you have difficulty in talking to your family member, see if someone else can, or hire a geriatric social worker to facilitate the discussion.

Fourth, ask family members what specifically they would like to do and are able to do. If one person loves to cook (and is good at it), lives nearby and wants to drop off meals three days a week, that is a no-brainer. If someone lives far away but has money to spare, paying for a home health aide would be a good fit. Teenage drivers in the family? Ask them to run errands or take their grandmother shopping. They will all be thrilled.

Finally, hire people to fill in the gaps. It may be more comfortable for your father to have a stranger help him bathe than to have you do it. Dog walkers can take care of the family pet so you do not have to run to the house every few hours. Grocery stores deliver. Most religious organizations have friendly visitors. Do not try to do everything yourself. It never works. It may seem to work in the very short term, but something always happens—the flu, an out-of-town meeting, a flat tire, and etcetera. Then, all the balls you have been juggling in the air fall down. Remember, the people who told you that you could have/do it all—have a great job, wonderful family, health, wealth and happiness—lied. They never had to drive carpool and conduct a major meeting at the same time they were picking up a sick kid from school and taking their mom to physical therapy.

E. What will not work:

1. Common situations that cause stress and general aggravation.

Poor Communication:
It all comes back to communication. DO not assume the child who lives closest to Mom and Dad should be the one who is primarily responsible for their care. Ask. If you are not the primary caregiver, ask what you can do to help. Be specific. Meaning, do not say, "Let me know if you need anything." Instead say, "Which day next week

would be best for you if I were to come and watch Mom?"Or, "I am going to the grocery store to pick up some food for Mom. Do you or she need anything else?"

Monday-Morning Quarterbacking:
Also, if you are not involved in the decision-making process, do not criticize the decisions. I cannot tell you how many times I have seen families torn apart when one sibling takes care of everything and the others play Monday-morning quarterback. It usually goes something like this...

Mom falls down on Sunday morning. The daughter who lives nearby (we will call her Katie), goes over to check on her mother on Sunday afternoon and finds her lying on the floor—where she has been all morning. Katie calls an ambulance, Mom goes to the hospital and finds out she broke her hip. The doctors tell Katie Mom will be in the hospital for a week or two and then will need rehabilitation. Katie calls her brother and sister to tell them what is going on and that she is concerned about Mom's moving back home after rehabilitation because she has to climb eight steps to get into the house and the bedroom is on the second floor. The siblings say, "Katie, you know the area, and you know Mom, and we trust you. Do what you think is best."So, she does. Usually, it takes a few weeks, but once the crisis is averted, the criticism comes. Either the family members question Katie's spending too much money on bringing a twenty-four hour aide into the house and getting a hospital bed so Mom can sleep downstairs, or they question why she did not do that and instead chose to help Mom move to a residential care facility.

Money:
Another situation involves money. Unfortunately, it is true that sometimes kids steal money from their elderly parents. However, it is not ALWAYS true. Meaning, look carefully before you accuse. This goes back to the meeting with the attorney, accountant and financial planner. Make sure you know who is in charge of the money and you trust them. If you do not, get a lawyer. There are all sorts of legal means to protect an elder and his/her assets, and an elder law attorney will know how to deal with them. Do not, however, try to be a lawyer yourself. See the section on elder abuse

in the appendices.

2. Family dynamics that do not work.

Ah, there is so much that does not work. This is the time when adult children not only have to deal with the current situation but also have to deal with all the baggage they have been carrying since childhood.

<u>"Dad was such a rotten father. I'm not going to help"</u>
This is not the time to argue about money, about the car, about who wants what jewelry, about who did more for Mom, about how Dad was never there when you had a baseball game, etcetera. I am not saying these feelings are not legitimate, but I am saying at this time it does not matter. Right now, your priority needs to be taking care of your elderly family member. So, if you are not able or willing to do so (and it is okay if you cannot), you need to find someone who can. Hire a professional and let them take care of everything.

<u>"I know what's best"</u>
On the other hand, there are children who think only they know what is best for Mom and Dad. They, under the guise or belief they are helping their parents, begin to isolate them from their other family members and friends. They will take care of everything themselves—even if it does not need to be done, even if things would be better if it were not done. I am sure you have stories of this on your own—the daughter who sells the one-level house and signs her mother-in-law up for assisted living while she is in the hospital, or the daughter who tries to have her father declared incompetent because he had an attorney (not his daughter) in charge of managing the money.

<u>"It's an emergency! I really need you!"</u>
Then, there is the how much do you love me game. It is really a way for a lonely family member to get more attention from his or her family. The sister game is "do not worry about me, I will just sit here alone in the dark". The first version is when the adult child calls his parents to see if he can pick anything up for them on his way over to visit. They need milk. So, he leaves work, picks up milk, stops at a deli to pick up lunch and drops by to visit his parents As he is getting ready to leave, his mother cries because even though the

refrigerator and freezer are full, there is nothing for dinner. So, the dutiful son goes back out to the grocery store and buys dinner. Of course, he asks if they need anything else before he goes, and they say "no" until he returns with the dinner and tries to leave to go back to work. Then, they need aspirin because they only have ten tablets left. Sound familiar?

The second version is when he calls to see what they need and they say, "Don't worry. We know you're busy with work, so we're just going to scrape the ice off the car and drive to the pharmacy for aspirin. We're down to the last ten tablets and that only will last a week. I only hope it's not too much for your mother's hip/father's heart." When he tries to protest that it is really not wise for them to shovel out the car and drive through an ice storm for aspirin they do not need today, he is met with a lot of arguments. Seem familiar?

The game really is the parent's way of saying they want to see their adult child. It is usually not about the aspirin. Some of my friends have been very successful by stocking up at the "big box" food clubs, and making sure there is always food in the refrigerator, easy-to-reheat meals in the freezer, extra medicine and bathing supplies. Then, they VISIT their parents as adult children, not errand runners—much more satisfactory for all involved. By the way, there are a lot of grocery stores, pharmacies and restaurants that deliver.

Again, it is not about money. It is not about jewelry. It is not about control. It is not about who is the best kid. It is about making sure the elderly family member is safe and well-cared-for.

The uncomfortable family dynamics are not unusual, and your family is not bad for experiencing them. However, when the dynamics take up more time than the caregiving, it is time to stop.

That is where the professionals come in.

3. Where to go for help
If you need someone to run interference among family members.

There are many, many, many people who can help you deal with these issues. First, call your employee assistance program (EAP).They understand that dealing with eldercare issues causes staff to be distracted from their jobs, and they should be able to refer you to counselors, social workers, or other professionals. Also, most faith-based social service agencies have trained professionals on staff who have seen this a million times before. So have members of the clergy. Finally, there are plenty of social workers who really understand the issues surrounding aging.

If your family member is in a nursing home, there usually are family councils. These can be a great support system.

The bottom line is—it is VERY tough to deal with aging issues, family dynamics, financial concerns and all the rest. Take advantage of the help that is available. Do not try to handle everything yourself—there's no need to.

D. Safety, safety, safety:

Perhaps the dementia patient should not still have his gun... I know

we are dealing with adults, and I know adults are not children. However, the same safety principles apply. You want to prevent injury as much as possible. So, while there are things you may be used to, you may want to re-think them.

1. Do not leave the car and house keys on the peg near the front door. Dementia patients can grab the keys, get in the car and drive away. Force of habit. You would be surprised what a dementia patient can do.

2. Do get the guns out of the house. I do not care if they are not loaded or the bullets are locked in another room. Someone with dementia may not recognize you, but may be able to load the gun. You never know—this is a very unpredictable disease.

3. Do put the knives away. Your uncle may not be a chef and may never have gone into the kitchen in his life. However, do you really trust that the man who no longer recognizes his family members will not take the nice, shiny knives off the magnetic bar in the kitchen or out of the knife block on the counter? Do you trust he will not hurt himself or someone else?

4. Do look at the stove and oven. Is it gas or electric? Where are the knobs? Watch how your family member uses the stove. Does s/he have to lean across hot burners to turn the stove on and off? If your family member has dementia, consider getting a child-proof lock for the oven controls. If it is gas, be sure to do so.

5. Do adjust the hot water heater. Remember older skin is more sensitive to being burned just as the senior's ability to recognize he or she is being burned decreases. The Shriner's Hospitals recommend lowering the thermostat setting of the water heater to 120-125 degrees Fahrenheit. They remind us "at 130 degrees, a serious burn can occur in thirty seconds. At 140 degrees, only five seconds are required. The time may be reduced by 50% or more for children under age five and some adults over sixty-five."

Consider installing shower/tub valves which reduce the water temperature to 115 degrees Fahrenheit or less. These valves can be attached to the bathtub fixtures, installed in the wall at the bathtub or connected at the water heater.

6. Do buy fire extinguishers for the kitchen and bedroom. While the best thing to do is have the senior leave the house and call 911 from outside the building, a fire extinguisher may buy some time as they try to reach the exit.

7. Do buy a carbon monoxide detector.

Remember, an ounce of prevention...

Chapter 2

Getting your ducks in a row: things you need to know before you look for help.

A. Medical Information:

1. What: a list of doctors, contact info, specialties and last time your family member saw him or her.

How: complete the checklist below.

Why: This information will help if your family member ever is hospitalized. The biggest reason, however, is that many people see many doctors who never talk to each other. So, you may have a primary care physician, cardiologist, endocrinologist, dentist and eye doctor who do not have a full picture of their patient. This does not make them bad doctors—it is a result of some pretty convoluted insurance plans and privacy issues. Later on, you will be reviewing which doctor prescribes which medication. You will be able to compare that list with this one to make sure your family member is not doctor-shopping or having issues of pain management not being taken seriously.

Doctor's first and last name	Address including city, state and zip AND EMAIL	Phone number	What kind of doctor?	Date of last visit	What did you see the doctor for?	Was this problem resolved?

2. What: a list of all medicines taken (prescription, herbal supplements and over-the-counter), dosage, when taken, who prescribed, for what.

How: Complete the checklist below (under the section about looking at the medicine).Also, open the medicine chest and cabinets to make sure you are not missing anything.

Why: Some medicines counteract each other, others can be harmful when taken together and still others cause side effects that mimic some pretty scary diseases. Still others exacerbate confusion, incontinence and more. Even over the counter (OTC) medicines need to be included. Finally, some herbal supplements/remedies interact very badly with traditional medicine. Since these supplements do not count as drugs and are therefore not regulated by the Food and Drug Administration (FDA) you need to be particularly careful when taking these.

3. What: actually open all the bottles and make a note of what the pills look like (be sure to note any identifying marks).

How: complete the checklist below.

Why: This is important for a number of reasons. First, you want to have a complete list to bring to every doctor each time your family member visits. Second, you want to be sure the medicines do not interact dangerously with each other, that any over-the-counter medicines are okay with the prescriptions and any herbal supplements are okayed by a physician. You also want to make sure the medicines are what they seem. As an example, sometimes the medicines come with child-proof caps that can be difficult to open. So, the patient moves the pills into another container. Now, the medicine is in a mislabeled container and it becomes easy to make mistakes.

Name of medicine	Dosage and how often it should be taken	Which doctor prescribed it?	What is it for?	Do you take it?	How long have you been taking it?	What does it look like?	When does it need to be refilled?

4. What: cross reference the list of doctors and medicines and see if it makes sense.

How: look at the checklist of doctors and the checklist of medicines. Is the primary care physician prescribing anti-depressants? Is the cardiologist doing the same? What about sleeping pills? Pain killers? Worse yet, is your family member self-medicating?

Why: This is important because you want to be sure the doctor who prescribed the medication is also monitoring it, ensuring the drugs are appropriate, do not interact badly and are being used as intended. **HELPFUL HINT: watch for doctor-shopping** (when the patient goes to multiple doctors for the same complaints) and for lack of coordination among the medical professionals. You should always have one doctor be the medical quarterback and coordinate all the medical plays.

5. Common issues with medication management
Taking medicine is complicated. Taking medicine when you do not feel well, cannot see the labels well or have trouble opening the packaging is even more difficult. This can result in the misuse of medicine—with potentially harmful or even fatal results. So, first

speak to one doctor and have him/her review all of the medicines, supplements and over-the-counter products. If he or she changes any of the medicines prescribed by another doctor, make sure to also check with that doctor before you implement any changes.

Then, once you have clearly understood what needs to be taken when, you will need to determine the best way for your family member to take the medicine. Would a chart or list help?

WHEN	WHICH MEDICINE DO I TAKE?	IS THIS EVERY DAY?IF NOT, LIST WHICH DAYS.
Before Breakfast		
With Breakfast		
After Breakfast		
Before Lunch		
With Lunch		
After Lunch		
Before Dinner		
With Dinner		
After Dinner		
Bedtime		

Would one of those plastic pill dispenser boxes help? Maybe a family member or nurse could put the pills in the box and clearly label the sections so it is easy to take. There are hundreds of designs to choose from.

What about one of the new, computerized pill dispensers? These range from inexpensive timers attached to small pill boxes to really fancy gadgets that do everything but walk over to the bed and put the pill in your mouth. Seriously, though, they have alarms, reminders, etcetera and actually dispense the medicine into a little cup. All you have to do is take the cup and swallow the pills. If you do not, it reminds you.

6. Other things to watch out for:
Okay. We have eliminated accidental or inadvertent medicine mismanagement. Now, let us deal with the more difficult issues—the situations that are not accidents.

a.   Cutting dosages in half or skipping them to save money. Tough problem, but there is a solution. There are prescription drug discount plans available.

One example is Together RX.(www.togetherrxaccess.com). This plan was started by some major pharmaceutical companies and offers discounts on over 150 commonly used medicines. It is a great plan for people with Medicare to explore. Basically, you fill out an application on-line and they send you a card which allows you to save 20% - 40% when you fill your prescriptions at most major pharmacies. It even covers some generic drugs. As of early 2004, they had over 1.3 million people using this service. They even have a special program for indigent elderly and will pre-load the card with cash to be used towards filling prescriptions.

A second example is the Medicare prescription drug program. More information is available at www.medicare.gov.

b.   Sharing prescriptions. You have seen it a million times. Friends gather around the pool, bingo table, etcetera and discuss their ailments. Someone always has a miracle cure—a magic pill. In the attempt to be caring and help his or her friends, the one who has the medicine (or herbal supplement) offers to share it. Just two words about this—DO NOT. What more can I say? It is dangerous and potentially life-threatening.

The second variation on this story is sharing antibiotics among family members .It is the old "I felt better so I stopped taking the antibiotic" story. I admit this one really makes me mad. Has no-one heard of antibiotic resistance? Just do not do it! Take your medicine and only your medicine. Finish it even if you feel better. The last thing anyone needs to do is to create bacteria that do not respond to antibiotics—especially in an older person whose immune system may already be weakened.

c.   Allergies. Maybe I should have put this first. If you are allergic to any medicines, make sure everyone knows. Get a Medic Alert bracelet. Put a note in your wallet or purse with the list of medicines you take. Fax it to your kids, doctors and best friend. The more people who know, the less likely you are to be given the drug.

d.   Herbal supplements. Do not take any herbal, natural or homeopathic remedy without checking with your **doctor** first. Never. Not even vitamins. Without extensive medical training, you cannot know whether or not the supplement will interact with medicine you are already taking or if it is safe. I cannot stress this enough. Just because the supplements or vitamins are marketed with a doctor's name on the label does not mean they are safe. Buyer beware and talk to your doctor.

B. Legal information:

1. Health care proxy: Health care proxies vary from state to state. Basically, this is a means for you to designate someone to make medical decisions for you should you be incapable of doing so. In some states, this person will also be able to donate your organs after you pass away. You should talk to your doctor about the rules in your state regarding who can make medical decisions for you if you cannot. Do not assume your family members automatically can—it is often not the case without a legal proxy. Some states, such as New York, do not require attorneys to complete these forms—you can do it yourself.

Here is a sample proxy for informational purposes only—make sure to use one authorized by your state.

1. I,_____hereby appoint

_____
(name, home address and telephone number)
as my health care agent to make any and all health care decisions for me, except to the extent that I state otherwise. This proxy shall take effect when and if I become unable to make my own health care decisions.

2. Optional instructions: I direct my agent to make health care decisions in accord with my wishes and limitations as stated below, or as he or she otherwise knows. (Attach additional pages if necessary.)

_____
_____

(Unless your agent knows your wishes about artificial nutrition and hydration (feeding tubes), your agent will not be allowed to make decisions about artificial nutrition and hydration. See instructions on reverse for samples of language you could use.)

3. Name of substitute or fill-in-agent if the person I appoint above is unable, unwilling or unavailable to act as my health care agent.

_____

(name, home address and telephone number)

_____

4. Unless I revoke it, this proxy shall remain in effect indefinitely, or until the date or conditions stated below. This proxy shall expire (specific date or conditions, if desired):

_____

5. Signature

_____

Address

_____

Date_____

Statement by Witnesses (must be eighteen or older)
I declare that the person who signed this document is personally known to me and appears to be of sound mind and acting of his or her own free will. He or she signed (or asked another to sign for him or her) this document in my presence.
Witness 1

_____

Address

_____

Witness 2

_____

Address

_____

2. Living will. Living wills also vary state by state .I suggest you consult an attorney to create one. Be aware, though, each state has its own requirements. You really do want a lawyer for this one. This ensures your medical wishes are carried out. Some common sense advice—even if you have a living will, make sure you tell your family what you want and believe in. Do not just say "no respirators"—do you really not want to be put on a respirator temporarily during surgery? Be clear. A very generic sample is below.

LIVING WILL

I,_____, of_____, being of sound mind, do hereby willfully and voluntarily make known my desire that my life not be prolonged under any of the following conditions, and do hereby further declare:

1. If I should, at any time, have an incurable condition caused by any disease or illness, or by any accident or injury, and be determined by any two or more physicians to be in a terminal condition whereby the use of "heroic measures" or the application of life-sustaining procedures would only serve to delay the moment of my death, and where my attending physician has determined that my death is imminent whether or not such "heroic measures" or life-sustaining measures are employed, I direct that such measures and procedures be withheld or withdrawn and that I be permitted to die naturally.

2. In the event of my inability to give directions regarding the application of life-sustaining procedures or the use of "heroic measures", it is my intention that this directive shall be honored by my family and physicians as my final expression of my right to refuse medical and surgical treatment, and my acceptance of the consequences of such refusal.

3. I am mentally, emotionally and legally competent to make this directive and I fully understand its import.

4. I reserve the right to revoke this directive at any time.

5. This directive shall remain in force until revoked.

IN WITNESS WHEREOF, I have hereto set my hand and seal this _____day of_____, 20___. Signed: ___

Declaration of Witnesses

The declarant is personally known to me and I believe him to be of sound mind and emotionally and legally competent to make the herein contained Directive to Physicians. I am not related to the declarant by blood or marriage, nor would I be entitled to any portion of the declarant's estate upon his decease, nor am I an attending physician of the declarant, nor an employee of the attending physician, nor an employee of a health care facility in which the declarant is a patient, nor a patient in a health care facility in which the declarant is a patient, nor am I a person who has any claim against any portion of the estate of the declarant upon his death.

Signed:_____ [6]

3. Durable power of attorney. Again, this varies from state to state. This basically gives you the chance to choose who has the ability to sign legal documents on your behalf should you become incapacitated. Once again, I urge you to hire an attorney for this one. You want to make sure it clearly represents your wishes.

4. Attorney's name and contact information. This one is pretty obvious, but make sure you know ALL attorneys who deal with your family members. Do not forget attorneys for any family-owned businesses.

5. Accountant's name and contact information. Again, pretty obvious, but necessary.

6. Insurance agents, policy numbers and contact information. Each insurance policy may have a different agent. Make sure you cover them all—health insurance, homeowner's, life, long-term care, etcetera.

7. Will. Yet another reason to hire an attorney. You want to make sure your treasured items go where you want them to. A clearly written will also eliminates a lot of infighting among family members.

8. Burial plans. Many seniors made these plans years ago. Find out the real deal: Is the funeral home still around? Is the cemetery still where they want to be buried? Have they already spent money for this?

9. Bank accounts, investment accounts. You want to make sure there is no hidden money you will not be able to find later on. Also, if you apply for financial assistance, you do not want it to appear as if you are hiding money.

10. Guardianship/conservatorship. There is a traditional distinction between a guardian who takes care of the healthcare, housing, food and daily living of a person who cannot take care of him or herself and a conservator who takes care of the financial end of things. However, this distinction sometimes gets fuzzy, especially when dealing with an elderly person who slowly is becoming incapacitated. This is yet one more time I would encourage you to hire an attorney.

Better yet, this is a great topic to raise when you have your team of legal and financial advisors together. For your information—some faith-based social service agencies have guardianship/conservatorship services available.

11. EMS forms. In many counties, the EMS (Emergency Medical Service) personnel are required to treat and transport to a hospital if 911 is called. Check with your county dispatcher (call the NON-emergency number to check) and see if they have a special form to allow you to specify which conditions/treatments are okay with you.

12. A "Dear Dummy" letter. I strongly suggest you write a clear letter saying, in plain English, what treatments are okay and what are not. Handwrite it CLEARLY or use a computer. It may have no legal standing, but it will help make your wishes clear. As an example, write that you, under no circumstances, want a feeding tube or that you want everything done to keep you alive. Whatever is important to you should be on this paper. Then, carry a copy in your purse or wallet and make sure your family members have copies, too. It may help to clear up any confusion and is a good supplement to the advanced directives and other legal documents.

13. MOLST/POLST forms.
Many states now have adopted standardized forms to address the end of life. Do not be fooled into thinking a do not resuscitate (DNR) order is all you need. There is a lot that can happen before you are unconscious and need to be resuscitated. Medical Orders

for Life Sustaining Treatment (MOLST) and Physician's Orders for Life Sustaining Treatment (POLST) forms address everything from DNR (do not resuscitate) to use of antibiotics, intubation and more. The best part is the forms need to be completed and signed by a physician, so it means you have professional guidance and an open conversation with someone who understands your medical condition and the results of the choices you make.

It is similar in concept to an advanced directive, but simpler and intended for medical professionals to use without having to read through multi-page legal documents. It is a great way to ensure your wishes are clear and easily followed.

Below is an example of a MOLST/POLST form. The legislation regulating the forms still is underway across the country, so the forms may change slightly, but the general gist will remain the same and still provide guidance to the medical professionals.

Medical Orders for Life-Sustaining		
Patient's Last Name, First, Middle Initial	Date of Birth	▢Male ▢Female
This form includes medical orders for Emergency Medical Services (EMS) and other medical personnel regarding cardiopulmonary (CPR) resuscitation and other life-sustaining treatment options for a specific patient. The physician must accurately and legibly complete the form and then sign and date it. A copy or the original of every completed MOLST/POLST form must be given to the patient or authorized decision maker within 48 hours of completion of the form or sooner if the patients discharged or transferred.		

CERTIFICATION FOR THE BASIS OF THESE ORDERS: Mark any and all that apply. Otherwise, leave this section blank. I hereby certify that these orders are entered as a result of a discussion with and the informed consent of:

_____the patient; or

_____the patient's healthcare agent as named in the patient's advance directive; or

_____the patient's guardian of the person; or

_____the patient's surrogate; or

_____if the patient is a minor, the patient's legal guardian or another legally authorized adult.

Or, I hereby certify that these orders are based on:

CPR (RESUSCITATION) STATUS:

_____**Attempt CPR:** If cardiac and/or pulmonary arrest occurs, attempt cardiopulmonary resuscitation (CPR). This will include any and all medical efforts that are indicated during arrest, including artificial ventilation and efforts to restore and/or stabilize cardiopulmonary function.

[If the authorized decision maker does not or cannot make any selection regarding CPR status, mark this option. Exceptions: If a valid advance directive declines CPR, CPR is medically ineffective, or there is some other legal basis for not attempting CPR, mark one of the —No CPRll options below.]

No CPR, Option A, Comprehensive Efforts to Prevent Arrest: Prior to arrest, administer all medications needed to stabilize the patient. If cardiac and/or pulmonary arrest occurs, do not attempt resuscitation (No CPR). Allow death to occur naturally.

_____**Option A-1, Intubate:** Comprehensive efforts may include intubation and artificial ventilation.

_____**Option A-2, Do Not Intubate (DNI):** Comprehensive efforts may include limited ventilatory support by CPAP or BiPAP, but do not intubate.

_____**No CPR, Option B, Palliative and Supportive Care:** Prior to arrest, provide passive oxygen for comfort and control any external bleeding. Prior to arrest, provide medications for pain relief as needed, but no other medications. Do not intubate or use CPAP or BiPAP. If cardiac and/or pulmonary arrest occurs, do not attempt resuscitation (No CPR). Allow death to occur naturally.

PHYSICIAN'S OR NURSE PRACTITIONER'S SIGNATURE (Signature and date are required to validate order)

Practitioner's Signature	Print Practitioner's Name	
License# and state licensed in	Phone Number	Date

_____Instructions in the patient's advance directive; or

_____Certification by two physicians that CPR and/or other specific treatments will be medically ineffective.

_____Mark this line if the patient or authorized decision maker declines to discuss or is unable to make a decision about these treatments. Participation in the preparation of the MOLST/POLST form is always voluntary. If the patient or authorized decision maker has not limited care, CPR will be attempted and other treatments will be given.

Patient's Last Name, First, Middle Initial	Date of Birth	
		☐Male ☐Female

Orders in Sections 2-9 below are for situations other than cardiopulmonary arrest.
Only complete applicable items in Sections 2 through 8, and only select one choice per applicable section.

ARTIFICIAL VENTILATION 2a._____May use intubation and artificial ventilation indefinitely, if medically intubation indicated. 2 2b._____May use intubation and artificial ventilation as a limited therapeutic trial. Time limit_ 2c.___May use on_____ indicated. ly CPAP or BiPAP for artificial ventilation, as medically Time limit_ 2d.___Do not use _____ any artificial ventilation (no ~~intubation~~, CPAP or BiPAP).	
BLOOD TRANSFUSION 3 3a._____May give any blood product (whole blood, packed red blood cells, plasma or platelets) that is medically indicated.	3b._____Do not give any blood products.

49

4	**HOSPITAL TRANSFER** 4a. ~~Transfer~~ to hospital for any situation requiring hospital-level care. _____	4b._____Transfer to hospital for severe pain or severe symptoms that cannot be controlled otherwise. 4c._____Do not transfer to hospital, but treat with options available outside the hospital.
5	**MEDICAL WORKUP** 5a. _____ May perform any medical tests indicated to diagnose and/or treat a medical condition. ____	5b. _____ Only perform limited medical tests necessary for symptomatic treatment or comfort. 5c.____ _____Do not perform any medical tests for diagnosis or treatment.
6	**ANTIBIOTICS** 6a. _____ May use antibiotics (oral, intravenous or intramuscular) as medically indicated. 6b. _____ May use oral antibiotics ~~when~~ medically indicated, but do not give intravenous or intramuscular antibiotics.	6c._____May use oral antibiotics only when indicated for symptom relief or comfort. 6d._____Do not treat with antibiotics.

7	**ARTIFICIALLY ADMINISTERED FLUIDS AND NUTRITION** 7a.__ _May give artificially administered fluids even indefinitely. 7b._____May give artificially administered fluids and nutrition, if medically indicated, asatrial. Time limit_____ 7c. _____May give fluids for artificially duration if medically indicated as the rapeutic trial, but do not give artificially administered nutrition. Time limit_ 7d. _____ Do not provide artificially administered fluids or nutrition.
8	**DIALYSIS** 8a._____May give chronic dialysis for end-stage kidney disease if medically indicated. 8b._____May give dialysis for a limited period. Time limit_____ 8c._____ Do not provide acute or chronic dialysis.

9 OTHER ORDERS		
PHYSICIAN'S OR NURSE PRACTITIONER'S SIGNATURE (Signature and date are required to validate order)		
Practitioner's Signature	Print Practitioner's Name	
License # and state in which issued	Phone Number	Date

For more information, ask your doctor, state department of health, or a local hospice agency. A word to the wise – some states require, or at least strongly suggest, the form be printed on bright pink paper.

C. Important family information:

1. <u>Know your family member's likes, dislikes and deal-breakers.</u> Is religion important to your family member? Then you better find a solution that includes regular visits from the member of the appropriate clergy. Does your mother like to be able to sit in a common area and socialize? Then you better find a place with lots of people around. Does your father hate cold weather? Look for someplace in a warmer climate. Make sure you clearly understand whether your family member is expressing a strong preference, wish or deal-breaker. In many cases, the religious affiliation of the organization is a deal-breaker. Make sure you find the right one.

2. <u>Be realistic about the time and resources each family member is willing and able to give.</u> Do not assume anything or pressure anyone. It never works. Quite frankly, no one owes anyone an explanation of why they are not willing to spend time or money others think they should. It is their choice, and there are many qualified, caring professionals who can provide the care. Also, be careful not to get caught in the guilt cycle.

3. <u>Evaluate the total support system</u> including friends, significant

51

others, relatives who are not immediate family members, religious organizations, etcetera. It is amazing how many friends you and your family members have. It is also amazing how many people do not ask for help. The easiest thing to do is make a list of all the people you would invite to a party if you won the lottery, won an all-expenses-paid cruise for one hundred people, etcetera. My theory is this: If you would be so quick to share your good fortune with these people, why not let them help you if you need it?

4. <u>Make sure there is support for the caregivers and other family members.</u> Remember the sick person is not the only one who needs help. I strongly recommend caregiver support groups or counseling. for anyone who needs it. Do not be ashamed. This is no time for heroics. Being strong is difficult, and we all could use a little boost now and then.

Aside from the support groups and counseling, I also mean support in the good friend kind of way. Here are some hints if you are NOT the primary caregiver. If you are making lasagna, make two and give one to the senior or the caregiver who may be too tired to make dinner for her kids. Send a card. Make a phone call. Take your friend out for a cup of coffee and let her whine. Laugh when it is funny and cry when it is not. Stop by the house on your way to the dry cleaner and pick up some dirty clothes. Drop it off when it is ready. With some of the new discount cleaners, you can be a real sport for twenty dollars.

Here are some hints if you ARE the primary caregiver. Let people help you. Call them if you have had a bad day and need to whine. Ask for help when you need it. Your good friends will still love you even if you break down in front of them. They will be mad if you needed help and never gave them the opportunity to help you.

D. Common sense stuff that drops by the wayside:

1. <u>Pets</u>. There are many residential care options that allow pets, so that should be your first choice. Maybe you can bring in a home health aide and hire a dog-walker or get a family member or friend whom the pet knows well to adopt him. Either way, understand the pet is extremely important to your family member. Studies have shown people with pets are calmer and happier than others. So, even if keeping the pet makes things a little more challenging, find a way to do it.

2. <u>Valuable items </u>(did Mom hide any money in the pages of the books? Jewelry in the freezer?).I have a friend whose mother has told everyone they should not throw out anything from her house when she dies unless it has been thoroughly inspected. She has admitted to hiding money between the pages of her books, hiding jewelry in places no one will be able to find it, and has still other things hidden in the pockets of her clothing. If your mom has done this, will you not feel terrible if you accidentally throw out her engagement ring? Perhaps you have heard the story about the woman who went on vacation and hid her jewelry in the freezer?

When she came back from vacation, she forgot. A few months later, she cleaned out her freezer. She did not remember she had hidden her jewelry and threw it out. She never got it back.

3. <u>The house:</u> Making sure it is properly maintained. Check the things you would usually check in your own home – the furnace, air conditioning, termites, roof, gutters, and etcetera. Air out the house once in a while. If you or your family members cannot keep it clean, hire someone to come in occasionally. Do not let the house deteriorate or become unsafe. If the house is completely uninhabited for a long time, stop the mail, put the lights on timers and do not leave the car in front of the house where it never moves. Have you thought about a house sitter or alarm system?

4. <u>The car. </u>This is a tough one. If the person is not ever going to drive it again, ask for their permission and sell it or give it away. Otherwise, make sure you do for this car what you do for your own. Also, do not leave the car in front of the house if you are not going to move it regularly—it is a big sign for thieves.

5. <u>The plants. </u>Someone needs to water them and feed them. If your family member cannot do it, ask the home health aide or a family friend to do it on a regular basis. Maybe you can hire someone to do the lawn and outside plants and ask them to take care of the inside ones too. You want to avoid having your family member come home to dead plants and an overgrown yard, or worse yet, sit at home and watch them die.

HELPFUL HINT: Check out www.lotsahelpinghands.com
This is a free, private, web-based community for organizing friends, family and colleagues who want to help you in your time of need. It allows users to easily coordinate activities and manage volunteers with an intuitive group calendar.

The "Lotsa" website points out the advantages of using their services:
"Everyone knows what to do and when to do it. Energy is spent helping, not scheduling.
Families in crisis are often overwhelmed with many offers of help and phone calls to return. If you are looking for ways to help a friend or loved one, you can create a private community to:

•   Organize well-meaning offers of help for meals delivery, rides and visits

•   Easily communicate and share updates using announcements, message boards and photos

•   Safely store vital information"[7]

Chapter 3

What types of solutions are there?

A. Home Health Agencies:

1. What do they do? Who do they serve?

Home health agencies provide HEALTH care. I stress this because many people confuse home health agencies with companionship services. While both types of care help people to stay at home, companions cannot bathe you, administer medicine or provide any real health care. They may call themselves in-home care or caregiver services but they are NOT the same thing as a home health care agency. So, be very specific when you speak to an agency that says it provides home care. If you need any assistance beyond what a regular person (meaning completely untrained in any medical field) can do, you want a home health care agency, not companion services. f you simply want some help with cooking and cleaning, a companion service is just fine. Either way, you will want to ask about the staff and their qualifications. Basically, a true home health care agency can help you with most of the activities of daily living such as bathing, cooking, toileting and also with assistance with medication and light housekeeping. They may have some restrictions such as being unable to lift a totally bedridden person, but they will usually tell you that in advance.

Home health care agencies often provide:

Skilled nursing care services: A level of care that must be given or supervised by registered nurses. Examples: getting intravenous injections, tube feeding, oxygen, changing sterile dressings on a wound.

Speech pathology services: This includes problems with speech, language and swallowing.

Physical therapy services: Treatment of injury and disease by mechanical means, such as heat, light, exercise and massage. Medical social services: These services assist with social and emotional concerns and may include counseling or help in finding resources in the community.

Occupational therapy: Services given to help return to usual activities such as bathing, preparing meals and housekeeping after illness either on an inpatient or outpatient basis.

Home health aide services: Services to help with daily living activities such as bathing, getting dressed, etcetera.

2. How do you know if they are good?

First, some definitions:

Accredited (accreditation): Is the home health agency accredited by The Joint Commission (JCAHO)? The Accreditation Commission for Home Care? CHAP (Community Health Accreditation Program)? This means the organization voluntarily sought accreditation and met national health and safety standards.

Licensed: Is the home health agency required to be licensed in your state? If so, are they? This means they have met certain standards set by a state or local government agency.

Certified (certification): If the home health agency is Medicare certified, it has passed an inspection survey done by a state government agency. Being certified is not the same as being accredited.

Background checks: It is extremely important that the agency conduct NATIONAL background checks on its employees. It is too easy to cross state lines and hide a criminal record. Do not compromise on this.

Before we get into the details about inspection reports and how to read them, I have a few disclaimers. First, while the agencies are evaluated by trained inspectors, please remember the inspectors are human, the patients/residents are human, and so are the staff at the organizations. Meaning, sometimes, people perceive things differently from each other. Furthermore, the quantitative standards used by Medicare only tell one side of the story. It is really hard to measure compassion and caring—very important characteristics in home health aides.

Basically, I urge you to use both Medicare reports as guidelines, not the Holy Grail. They are extremely valuable tools in helping you determine the general level of quality of the facility. They tell you where the problems have occurred and how responsive the provider was in fixing the problems.

It is vital, however, that you think about what you are reading and evaluate whether or not a deficiency really presents a problem. Medicare does "risk adjust" to ensure agencies that serve older, frailer residents do not have much worse scores than those serving primarily "younger elderly".

3. How do you find and understand a Medicare report?

Be aware: The list of home health agencies is based on the places where they have provided services in the past. If the provider was bought or changed management, the report may not be entirely accurate.

First, go to www.medicare.gov.
Then, under "doctors, providers, hospitals, & plans" look for "find home health services."Remember, this only is for Medicare certified home health care agencies, not companion care or those that do not accept Medicare.

You can search by zip code, city and state, name and more. The website is well-designed and pretty easy to understand.

Once you search, you will be shown a list of care providers that match your criteria. It will show you which services each provider offers and their contact information.

When you click on the agency's name, you will see the type of ownership, year it became Medicare certified and a detailed report of the agency's performance. At this time, the Medicare website allows you to compare a particular agency against both state and national average performances.

Now, here is the ugly reality. Agencies often are evaluated on factors that are not always relevant, so again, use these reports as a guide, not as the Holy Grail. For example, one of the evaluation factors is "how often patients get better at..." Rehabilitation patients should show improvement in (get better at) some things. Other, older, frailer, sicker adults are not necessarily going to improve or get better. So, these percentages sometimes do not make much sense.

I do, however, watch the pain management scores. It is a personal crusade of mine to make sure older adults have their pain taken seriously and treated.

Also, the unplanned hospital care is a tricky one. Prevention is important, but we cannot prevent everything. Some older adults want to be taken to the hospital while others prefer only palliative care. So, this category presents some challenges.

The bottom line is that the Medicare scores can show you:
- the provider really is certified by Medicare.
- the outliers—the agencies that are significantly better or worse than average.

That is it, though You really need to become an educated consumer in order to make the best decisions.

4. How do you find and understand a Joint Commission (JCAHO) report?

First, a brief explanation of JCAHO.

Mission: To continuously improve health care for the public, in collaboration with other stakeholders, by evaluating health care organizations and inspiring them to excel in providing safe and effective care of the highest quality and value.

Vision: All people always experience the safest, highest quality, best-value health care across all settings.

Founded in 1951, The Joint Commission seeks to continuously

improve health care for the public, in collaboration with other stakeholders, by evaluating health care organizations and inspiring them to excel in providing safe and effective care of the highest quality and value. The Joint Commission evaluates and accredits more than nineteen thousand health care organizations and programs in the United States. An independent, not-for-profit organization, The Joint Commission is the nation's oldest and largest standards-setting and accrediting body in health care. To earn and maintain The Joint Commission's Gold Seal of Approval™, an organization must undergo an on-site survey by a Joint Commission survey team at least every three years. (Laboratories must be surveyed every two years.)[8]

To evaluate a care provider, go to www.jointcommission.org

In the action center, look for "find an accredited organization."You can search by name, organization number, state or zip code.

Please note this is a voluntary accreditation. Some very good providers are not accredited.

Searching for and clicking on a provider tells you the certification status of the provider and the quality check section of the website is also good to help compare a particular provider against state and national standards.

5. How do you find and read a Community Health Accreditation Program (CHAP) report?

Go to www.chapinc.org—accreditation, accredited agency locator.

You can search by agency name, state, etcetera.

Again, please note this is a voluntary accreditation, and some very good providers are not accredited.

The report tells you the accreditation status, date and services offered.

6. What questions should you ask?

So, you know how to evaluate the quantitative information about a home health care provider. You can tell how a particular provider compares to others. Now for the hard part. How will this particular care provider fit into your family's life?

Let's say you have determined your mother needs help managing her diabetes. She needs someone to give her insulin injections, make sure she is eating properly, etcetera. She also needs someone to help her bathe, help with cooking and do some light housekeeping and laundry. You find the perfect person—a nurse with an accredited agency that has excellent survey results. The nurse is licensed, insured, has passed her background check, is talented, capable and kind, and your mother hates her. Your mother fires her.

Can this be avoided? Maybe not. It may just be that your mother is going to hate everyone who comes into her house to make her take her medicine. I still remember when we paid a home health aide to help my grandfather bathe. We could not understand why my grandfather was not clean when we visited—even if it was the same day the aide came. Turned out, my grandfather refused to let the aide bathe him.

So, what can you do? Once you do the obvious—checking the licensing, inspection results and staff qualifications— you need to ask the really tough questions.

First, start with your family member.

Will he or she let someone come into the house to provide care? If not, what does he or she suggest? Having you do everything is not a solution unless you are a trained medical professional. So, nip this one in the bud.

Will they let someone else see them naked? If he or she needs assistance with bathing, this is something you will need to address before the aide gets there. What about a nurse of the opposite gender? We all know these people are trained medical professionals and are used to seeing people's bodies, but that does not matter if your mom will not take off her clothes. If this is an issue, ask your family member what they are willing to do. There has to be some acceptable compromise—it is your job to find it.

Does your family member speak English as a foreign language? If his or her grasp of English is not strong, you should try to find a home health aide who speaks the same language. You want to eliminate any chances of miscommunication. On the same note, you want to make sure the aide can speak English fairly well. This person is going to be spending a lot of time with your family member. They have to be able to communicate.

Does your family member have strong preferences about smoking? While no self-respecting home health aide will smoke in a patient's house, if they smoke, their clothes still will smell. If this is something that bothers your family member, be up front about it.

Does your family member have strong preferences about food or meals? If so, tell the home health aide up front. If you keep Kosher or are a vegetarian, be sure to let the agency know if the aide will not be able to bring food into the house.

Finally, and most importantly, be sure to tell the agency about your family member's personality. This prevents a lot of problems up front. Meaning, if your dad is shy and formal, he most likely will not like a young, gum-chewing aide with a cropped shirt and pierced belly button who calls him "Pops" no matter how good she is at her job. On the other hand, your talkative mother might really like her.

7. What about home health care supplies?

There is always a question about providing supplies. You can run yourself ragged and spend a fortune chasing down supplies such as geriatric diapers, wipes, lotion, tissues, canes and walkers. Very often, the home health agency can provide some of the items—sometimes it will not cost you anything out-of-pocket. Obviously, if it is free to you and they are willing to provide it—SAY YES.

However, if you need to supply the items yourself, it can be a real pain. These items are expensive. Pharmacies and grocery stores are very expensive. Medical supply stores are a little cheaper.

8. How to make your home safer:

- Install grab bars in the shower, tub, and near the toilet. Consider installing raised toilet seats with handles on the sides.
- Put nightlights in the bathroom and kitchen. Studies have shown that seniors fall more often in low-light environments, but they do not want to turn on the overhead light and wake their spouse. Keep flashlights everywhere. Again, low-light can be a problem. Only use non-skid mats.
- Make a box of emergency supplies. Get a first aid kit.
- Install a carbon monoxide detector. Check smoke detectors regularly.
- Purchase or rent emergency call buttons or some other home monitoring system.
- Make sure there is a peephole in the front door or some way to see who is there before you open the door.
- Do not have cords of any sort lying on the floor—they are too easy to trip over.

Independent living/ retirement communities:

1. What do they do? Who do they serve?

Generally, independent living and retirement communities provide meals, housekeeping, transportation, social and recreational activities and laundry. While they traditionally do not provide health services or personal care, many communities will allow you to contract with a home health agency and receive these services. Still others will provide these services for an additional fee. Quite frankly, as the residents of independent living communities have gotten older and aged-in-place, the communities have had to add services to meet their needs. Consequently, the line between independent living and assisted living has blurred.

2. How do you know if they are good?

This is a tough one. It is not like you can pick up an inspection report and see how well they scored on *percentage of patients who got better at…* as you can for a home health agency or a nursing home. There are requirements for things like inspections by the department of health, fire marshal, and others, however. If I were looking for an independent living or retirement community, I would ask the administration of the particular community who licenses them and ask to see any inspection reports available. The requirements vary state by state, so I would also contact your state's department of elder services and ask if they have any particular suggestions or concerns.

Then, I would visit the community and ask a lot of questions. Suggestions are below.
3. What questions should you ask?

The trick is to find the good independent living community that makes your family member happy and provides good health care if it becomes necessary. If they cannot provide the care if or when it becomes necessary, your family member will have to move unless the community allows you to pay separately for a home health aide.

Let us start with the health care side first:
What services does the community provide? Ask specific, detailed questions. Some suggestions are below:

Do they have staff who can supervise medication? What EXACTLY can they do to supervise the medication? Can they open the pill bottle and hand your family member the pill? Can they open the pill bottle but your family member has to get the pill out of the bottle him or herself? Can they not even open the bottle? I know this seems silly, but someone who has arthritis or a weak grip may have trouble opening the bottles. Also, some people lack the dexterity to get the pills out of the bottle. Different care providers have different kinds of licenses which may not allow them to even touch the pill bottles.

How many meals do they provide daily? Weekends? Snacks? Can you pay extra to get more meals? What about purchasing meals for guests?

If someone is sick and cannot make it to the dining room, will someone bring a meal to his or her apartment? How much extra does this cost? Is there a limit to how often they will do it?

What are the emergency medical procedures? I do not mean "is there a call button". I mean, if there is a medical emergency with your family member, what exactly does the facility do? Calling 911 is an obvious answer. What, if anything, do they do beyond that?

Will they provide transportation to or from doctor appointments?

How is the organization staffed on a regular basis? During evenings and weekends? How many nurses are on duty?

Is there access to a medical staff of board-certified geriatricians? Consulting specialists? Nurse practitioners? While the facilities may not provide the care themselves, some actually have partnered with medical practices that have offices on-site.

Are there any routine medical services and facilities available on-site (for example x-rays, dental, auditory testing)?

Does the organization have an affiliation with any medical schools or clinical research programs?

How are medical situations handled if they are beyond the organization's capabilities? If a resident needs to go to the hospital or a specialist, are they accompanied by a staff member from the organization?

Does the organization offer physical, occupational and other therapies? How often?

Do not forget the social side of the equation.

B. Assisted Living:

While assisted living is a great concept, the implementation varies so widely, you need to be incredibly thorough in your analysis and research.

There are some truly outstanding care providers in assisted living— but it is really hard for a consumer to determine which ones are best. It gets even more difficult when each state has a different name for assisted living. Synonyms include: personal care homes, boarding homes, residential care facilities, adult homes and homes for the aged.

While there are outstanding care providers, there also are inexcusable, disgusting, unsafe places. I am sure you have seen the articles in major newspapers about the horrible care provided. There have been stories of sexual predators being released from jail and housed in assisted living facilities while they rehabilitate. Some facilities house both elderly and younger people where the elderly are frail and the young are strong and are drug users who need to go through detox. Some are criminals. Some are mentally ill.

Yes, those horrible places do exist, but there are some truly outstanding ones that provide excellent care. The challenge is in how to know the difference.

It basically comes down to this... The individual consumer has to take a lot of responsibility to ensure the organization can and is providing the best care possible. In this chapter, I will provide you with the tools you need to make an educated decision.

1. What do they do?

Essentially, assisted living facilities take care of people who cannot live alone and do not need twenty-four hour skilled nursing care. The residents need help with the activities of daily living. Yes, I know this is a generic definition, but since the definitions and standards vary from place to place, it is the best I can do.

Why assisted living? If an older adult needs help with bathing, cooking, shopping, etcetera, he or she has three choices—relying on family or friends, hiring a home health aide, or moving to some residential community that has care available. Here is where it gets tricky, though. Some independent living communities have supportive services such as community meals, housekeeping and linen service. Still other independent living/retirement communities allow you to pay extra for a home health aide to provide services within their community—then they look like assisted living facilities. Some assisted living facilities allow you to bring in a nurse for additional care—then they look like nursing homes. So, it all becomes a blur.

Here is how I look at it. If your family member needs some help with activities of daily living and can get in and out of his or her house easily, has plenty of social interaction with friends, family and neighbors, then a home health aide is fine. If, however, the person is socially and physically isolated, lonely and/or bored, it is time to look at residential care.

Assisted living is a HUGE industry. According to the United States General Accounting Office (GAO), in 2002 there were over thirty-six thousand assisted living facilities serving approximately nine-hundred thousand residents. Each state is responsible for regulating its own assisted living providers.

In general, the typical assisted living resident is:
- between seventy-five and eighty-five
- female (more than two-thirds of the residents are female)
- 25% of the residents need help with more than three activities of daily living
- 86% require or accept help with their medication[9]

2. How do you know if they are good?

After receiving the Assisted Living Workgroup's report, the Senate Special Committee on Aging asked the GAO to review state efforts in three selected areas. In April, 2004, the United States General Accounting Office (GAO) issued a report reviewing the assisted living industry and highlighting some particular state initiatives addressing consumer protection.

They reviewed three specific areas of the assisted living industry:
1. disclosure of full and accurate information by the assisted living facility to consumers.
2. state assistance to help care providers meet licensing requirements.
3. procedures for addressing residents' complaints.

What did they find? They found that "Consumers often lack key information to make appropriate choices."[10] Even less surprising than that finding, they discovered consumers often were given incomplete or misleading information.

The good news is they found five specific initiatives in Florida, Texas, Washington, Georgia and Massachusetts that differ from typical approaches and could serve as models for other states.

If I were looking for an assisted living facility, I would first get a copy of the appropriate state regulations and read them. I know, they are complicated and often boring, but you need to have a basic idea of what the regulations require/allow. You can ask your state's office of elder affairs where to find these regulations. Their eldercare ombudsman also is a good resource.

3. What questions should you ask?

The trick is to find the good assisted living community that makes your family member happy and provides good health care.

Let us start with the health care side first:
What services does the community provide? Ask specific, detailed questions. Some suggestions are below:

Will they bathe your mother? How often?

Administer the medicine or just supervise her when she takes it? Again, ask for specific details. Can they open the pill bottle? Hand the pills to the resident?

How many meals do they provide daily? Weekends? Can you pay extra to get more meals?

If someone is sick and cannot make it to the dining room, will someone bring a meal to his or her apartment? How much extra does this cost? Is there a limit to how often they will do it? What about guest meals?

What are the emergency medical procedures? Specifics here too. What do they do other than dial 911?

Will they provide transportation to and from doctor appointments?

How is the organization staffed during evenings and weekends?

How many nurses are on duty? What kind of nurses? Doctors?

Is there a medical staff of board-certified geriatricians? Consulting specialists? Nurse practitioners?

What routine medical services and facilities are available on-site (for example x-rays, dental, auditory testing)?

Does the organization have an affiliation with any medical schools or clinical research programs?
How are medical situations handled if they are beyond the organization's capabilities? If a resident needs to go to the hospital or a specialist, are they accompanied by a staff member from the organization?

Does the organization offer physical, occupational and other therapies? How often?

Does the organization's dementia special care unit provide a physical environment that is specially designed for the safety of the residents?

C.   Nursing Homes:

Long-term care services:
Long-term care services are provided by nursing facilities that offer twenty-four hour nursing or rehabilitative care. Long-term care centers—nursing homes, skilled nursing facilities (SNFs), or long term care facilities—provide short-term and/or residential care. Some residents may be discharged to their home or to an assisted living community.

People often are misinformed about Medicare, Medicaid, what they are, what they pay for, rules for eligibility and more. Check out www.medicare.gov for a complete explanation.

1.   What do nursing homes do?
Nursing homes generally provide twenty-four hour medical care, room and board, activities, and more. They are intended for people who really do need twenty-four hour medical care, not people who just need help with activities of daily living. Care is described as

fitting into one of the two categories below. Please be aware that these definitions vary somewhat depending on the insurance provider, etcetera.

<u>Custodial Care</u> (non-skilled):Assistance with activities of daily living including bathing, eating, dressing, toileting, transferring from the bed to a wheelchair, etcetera. This is the type of care that can safely be provided by non-medical personnel. Generally, however, people who need this type of care and choose nursing home over other care options also need some sort of regular medical care.
<u>Skilled Nursing</u>: Includes care that must be provided by or supervised by qualified technical or professional staff such as registered nurses, licensed nurses, physical therapists, occupational therapists and speech pathologists or audiologists. Examples include the administration of intravenous feedings and intramuscular injections, the insertion of catheters and ultrasound therapy treatments. Basically, if the task could be safely done by a non-medical person, it is not skilled nursing. It is important to note that skilled services may be provided even if the patient's full or partial recovery is not expected. Meaning, these services may be provided only to ensure the patient does not get worse. Patients with terminal illnesses still may receive skilled care to alleviate pain, etcetera.

2. How do you know if they are good?

The Basics:

Does the organization accept payment from Medicare and Medicaid? Medicare certification means the organization has met the minimum health and safety requirements established by the federal government. For eligible residents, Medicare and Medicaid will provide reimbursement only for services offered by a certified agency.

Will the organization provide you with a written description of its services and fees? What resources will the organization provide to help you find financial assistance if it is needed?

Does the organization have an emergency plan in place? In the case of an emergency, can the organization continue to provide care? If it cannot, how will care be provided? Is there a plan to notify residents' families in case of a general emergency?

Definitions:

Accredited (accreditation): Is the nursing home accredited by the Joint Commission on the Accreditation of Healthcare Organizations (JCAHO)?
This means the organization voluntarily sought accreditation and met national health and safety standards. Please be aware that some of the huge long-term care organizations that offer a wide range of services may have chosen not to become JCAHO accredited because their range of services is structured so differently than the average provider. They still are outstanding.

Licensed: Are the nursing home and current administrator required to be licensed in your state? If so, are they? This means that they have met certain standards set by a state or local government agency.

Certified (certification): If the nursing home is Medicare and Medicaid certified, the nursing home has passed an inspection survey done by a state government agency. Medicare and Medicaid will only pay for care in a certified nursing home. Being certified is not the same as being accredited. Please be aware some nursing homes set aside only a few beds for Medicare or Medicaid residents. I would not be surprised if some providers stop accepting Medicare since there is an issue of the reimbursement rates being too low for the nursing homes to stay in business. At that point, they no longer would have Medicare inspection results. For now, however, Medicare certification still is a good quality indicator.

Disclaimers: Before we get into the details about inspection reports and how to read them, I have a few disclaimers. First, while the facilities are evaluated by trained inspectors, please remember the inspectors are human, the patients and residents are human, and so are the staff at the organizations. Meaning, sometimes, people perceive things differently from each other. Furthermore, the quantitative standards used by Medicare only tell one side of the story. Yes, you can compare the occurrence of pressure ulcers (commonly known as bedsores) from one facility to another. However, it can be very difficult—perhaps impossible—to know whether the resident or patient developed a pressure ulcer while in the facility, or arrived to the facility already having one.

Basically, I urge you to use both Medicare and Joint Commission reports as guidelines, not the Holy Grail. They are extremely valuable tools in helping you to determine the general level of quality of the facility. They tell you where problems have occurred, and how responsive the facility was in fixing the problem.

It is vital, however, you think about what you are reading and evaluate whether or not a deficiency really presents a problem. Remember that in general the population of a nursing home is very frail.

Also, take into account that some of the deficiencies may really be clerical errors or paperwork issues, not direct care issues. I remember hearing a story of an outstanding nursing home that was cited for not immediately producing documentation when the inspector arrived. Why did they not? The facility had survived an earthquake less than twelve hours before and the staff was busy ensuring the residents were okay and working with structural engineers to make sure the facility was safe. Obviously, they made the right choice to deal with safety and security rather than re-filing paperwork that fell during the earthquake, but they still got dinged.

Having said that, let us explore facility reports...

3. How to read a Medicare inspection report

Go to www.medicare.gov and click on *find doctors, providers, hospitals, & plans*. Then, click on *find nursing homes*. Medicare updates its website on a regular basis, so the steps may change, but the nursing home comparison tool will be somewhere on their website.

The tools for finding a nursing home are pretty intuitive. One word of caution—while it is tempting to emphasize your convenience and choose a nursing home based on geography, be careful. I understand you may want to be close to the nursing home so you can visit often, but please remember your loved one is living there twenty-four, seven. Do not compromise care for convenience if you do not have to.

Also, please be aware that hospital discharge planners usually refer to the closest rehabilitation facilities. Again, do not compromise care for convenience if you do not have to. Medicare offers many choices.

Now, let us explore what Medicare analyzes for you.

Medicare currently uses a five star system to rate nursing homes.

Much Above Average   *****

Above Average   ****

Average   ***

Below Average   **

Much Below Average   *

When you use the search process on the Medicare website, you will be shown a list of providers that meet your criteria. You will see the five-star system used for overall rating, health inspections, nursing home staffing and quality measures. You will also see whether the nursing home participates in Medicaid or not. Finally, you will see the number of beds and ownership.

Medicare offers detailed explanations of each of these categories. Here is an example of a report taken in 2011. The format of the reports may change over time, but the general gist remains the same.

Health Inspections   4 out of 5 stars
Lists the health requirements that the nursing home failed to meet in the last 3 years.

Date of last standard health inspection: 05/13/2011

Dates of Complaint Investigations: 06/01/2010 - 08/31/2011
Total number of Health Deficiencies for this nursing home: 8

Average number of Health Deficiencies in Virginia: 8

Average number of Health Deficiencies in the United States: 8

Range of Health Deficiencies in Virginia: 0-

How to Read a Health / Fire Safety Deficiency Chart

Quality Care Deficiencies

Inspectors determined that the nursing home failed to:	Inspection Date	Date of Correction	Level of Harm (Least -> Most)	Residents Affected (Few -> Some -> Many)
1. Give each resident care and services to get or keep the highest quality of life possible.	05/13/2011	07/22/2011	2 = Minimal harm or potential for actual harm	Few
2. Give professional services that meet a professional standard of quality.	05/13/2011	07/22/2011	2 = Minimal harm or potential for actual harm	Few
3. Give residents proper treatment to prevent new bed (pressure) sores or heal existing bed sores.	05/13/2011	07/22/2011	3 = Actual harm	Few
Resident Assessment Deficiencies				
Inspectors determined that the nursing home failed to:	Inspection Date	Date of Correction	Level of Harm (Least -> Most)	Residents Affected (Few -> Some -> Many)

73

4. Develop a complete care plan that meets all of a resident's needs, with timetables and actions that can be measured.	05/13/2011	07/22/2011	2 = Minimal harm or potential for actual harm	Few
Resident Rights Deficiencies				
Inspectors determined that the nursing home failed to:	Inspection Date	Date of Correction	Level of Harm (Least -> Most)	Residents Affected (Few -> Some -> Many)
5. Immediately tell the resident, doctor, and a family member if: the resident is injured, there is a major change in resident's physical/mental health, there is a need to alter treatment significantly, or the resident must be transferred or discharged.	05/13/2011	07/22/2011	2 = Minimal harm or potential for actual harm	Few
Pharmacy Service Deficiencies				
Inspectors determined that the nursing home failed to:	Inspection Date	Date of Correction	Level of Harm (Least -> Most)	Residents Affected (Few -> Some -> Many)
6. 1) Make sure that residents who take drugs are not given too many doses or for too long; 2) make sure that the use of drugs is carefully watched; or 3) stop or change drugs that cause unwanted effects.	05/13/2011	07/22/2011	2 = Minimal harm or potential for actual harm	Few
7. At least once a month, have a licensed pharmacist	05/13/2011	07/22/2011	2 = Minimal harm or	Few

check the drugs that each resident takes.			potential for actual harm	

Environmental Deficiencies

Inspectors determined that the nursing home failed to:	Inspection Date	Date of Correction	Level of Harm (Least -> Most)	Residents Affected (Few -> Some -> Many)
8. Have a program to keep infection from spreading.	05/13/2011	07/22/2011	2 = Minimal harm or potential for actual harm	Few

	Nursing Home Staffing Information comes from data that the nursing home reports to its state agency. It contains the nursing home staffing hours for a two- week period prior to the time of the state inspection. CMS receives this data and converts it into the number of staff hours per resident per day.	4 out of 5 stars

Nursing Home Staff	National Average	Average in Virginia	Home example
RN Staff Only[1]	Not Available	Not Available	4 out of 5 stars
Total Number of Residents	93	145	60
Total Number of Licensed Nurse Staff Hours per Resident per Day	1 hour 24 minutes	1 hour 48 minutes	2 hours 10 minutes
RN Hours per Resident per Day	36 minutes	42 minutes	50 minutes
LPN/LVN Hours per Resident per Day	48 minutes	1 hour 6 minutes	1 hour 20 minutes
CNA Hours per Resident per Day	2 hours 24 minutes	2 hours 48 minutes	2 hours 49 minutes

- How to Read a Staffing Chart
- About Staff Roles

[1] The star rating a nursing home received for the information it provided about its Registered Nurse (RN) staffing. RNs have between 2 and 6 years of education.

Quality Measures Information comes from data that the nursing homes regularly report on all residents. It		4 out of 5 stars
includes aspects of residents' health, physical functioning, mental status and general wellbeing.		

Quality Measures	National Average	Average in Virginia	Home example
Long-Stay Residents			
NOTE: For the following measures, **higher percentages are better.**			
Percent of long-stay residents given influenza vaccination during the flu season	92%	87%	98%
Percent of long-stay residents who were assessed and given pneumococcal vaccination	90%	77%	97%
NOTE: For the following measures, **lower percentages are better.**			
Percent of long-stay residents whose need for help with daily activities has increased	14%	11%	7%
Percent of long-stay residents who have moderate to severe pain	3%	0%	0%
Percent of high-risk long-stay residents who have pressure sores	11%	12%	6%
Percent of low-risk long-stay residents who have pressure sores	2%	2%	Not Available
Percent of long-stay residents who were physically restrained	3%	1%	1%
Percent of long-stay residents who are more depressed or anxious	14%	6%	10%
Percent of low-risk long-stay residents who lose control of their bowels or bladder	51%	60%	62%
Percent of long-stay residents who have/had a catheter inserted and left in their bladder	5%	3%	2%

Percent of long-stay residents who spend most of their time in bed or in a chair	4%	2%	5%
Percent of long-stay residents whose ability to move about in and around their room got worse	11%	10%	13%
Percent of long-stay residents who had a urinary tract infection	9%	7%	10%
Percent of long-stay residents who lose too much weight	8%	8%	5%

Short-Stay Residents

NOTE: For the following measures, **higher percentages are better.**

Percent of short-stay residents given influenza vaccination during the flu season	85%	65%	96%
Percent of short-stay residents who were assessed and given pneumococcal vaccination	84%	54%	84%

NOTE: For the following measures, **lower percentages are better.**

Percent of short-stay residents who have delirium	1%	1%	1%
Percent of short-stay residents who had moderate to severe pain	19%	8%	11%
Percent of short-stay residents who have pressure sores	12%	16%	14%

Fire Safety Inspections
Lists the fire safety requirements that the nursing home failed to meet. Fire safety results are not included in the nursing home's Overall Rating.

Automated Sprinkler Systems in all required areas	Fully Sprinklered
Date of last standard fire safety inspection:	05/18/2011
Dates of Complaint Investigations:	06/01/2010 - 08/31/2011
Total number of Fire Safety Deficiencies for this nursing home:	1
Average number of Fire Safety Deficiencies in Virginia:	2

Average number of Fire Safety Deficiencies in the United States:	4
Range of Fire Safety Deficiencies in Virginia:	0 - 19

Miscellaneous Deficiencies

Inspectors determined that the building did not have:	Inspection Date	Date of Correction	Level of Harm (Least -> Most)	Residents Affected (Few -> Some -> Many)
1. fire safety features required by current fire safety codes.	05/18/2011	07/13/2011	2 = Minimal harm or potential for actual harm	Few

	Penalties and Denials of Payment Against the Nursing Home Lists the civil monetary penalties and payment denials that the nursing home received in the last 3 years.		
Penalties and Denials of Payment Against the Nursing Home		Date	Amount
This Nursing Home has not been cited for any Enforcement Actions in the last 3 years.			
	Complaints and Incidents Lists the deficiencies from incidents reported by the nursing home in the last 3 years as well as complaints.		

What you need to know about reading these reports:
Care providers and inspectors are human and no place is perfect. The data only tells part of the story—it certainly can tell you a terrible place is terrible or an excellent place is excellent IN THE AREAS THAT ARE ANALYZED.

Also, remember the social factors—will your loved one be happy, safe and comfortable with the particular provider? It is not just about medical care.

Many care providers also are accredited by the Joint Commission.

4.   What is a Joint Commission report? How do you read it?

The Joint Commission on Accreditation of Healthcare Organizations(often still referred to as JCAHO, pronounced "Jayco") is an independent, not-for-profit organization, established over fifty years ago.JCAHO is governed by a board that includes physicians, nurses and consumers and evaluates the quality and safety of care for nearly seventeen-thousand health care organizations. To maintain and earn accreditation, organizations must have an extensive on-site review by a team of JCAHO health care professionals at least once every three years. The purpose of the review is to evaluate the organization's performance in areas that affect your care. Accreditation may then be awarded based on how well the organizations met JCAHO standards.[11]

Go to www.qualitycheck.org to open a search window that allows you to look for accredited organizations.

It then allows you to look for a particular service or provider through the Quality Check program and download a .pdf report that shows how well the provider meets Joint Commission standards.

Again, this is a useful tool, but does not cover everything you need to know.

5. What questions should you ask?

In addition to the inspection results and survey results from Medicare and/or JCAHO, there are some questions you the consumer need to ask. Make sure you are comfortable with the answers. Your needs may be different than the next family's—and the answers are more qualitative than quantitative. Remember, a facility that has outstanding inspection and survey results may not necessarily be the best fit for your family member. I am not saying you want to go to a place that provides bad care, but one that has a minor deficiency but still meets all of your other qualifications should stay in the running.

Determining what the resident needs:

Does a qualified staff member conduct a preliminary evaluation of the resident's needs? Can you be involved in this evaluation? Does

the organization create a plan of care for each new resident? Will you be involved in establishing the plan of care?
Find out whom you need to contact or who will contact you when this plan changes.

Does the organization provide the specific services you or your family member need?

The medical side of the equation:
The bottom line is… is the medical care the best available?

This is where the JCAHO and Medicare reports come in. How does the facility compare to others? Are you comfortable with their inspection results?

How is the organization staffed during evenings and weekends? How many nurses are on duty? What is the ratio of nurses' aides (CNAs) to residents? Is a physician available at all times?

Is there a full-time medical staff of board-certified geriatricians? Consulting specialists? Nurse Practitioners?

What routine medical services and facilities are available on-site (for example, x-rays, dental, auditory testing)?

What is the organization's ability to diagnose and treat residents' chronic or acute conditions without transferring to hospitals or other diagnostic facilities?

Does the organization have an affiliation with any medical schools or clinical research programs?

How are medical situations handled if they are beyond the organization's capabilities? If a resident needs to go to the hospital or a specialist, are they accompanied by a staff member from the organization?

Does the organization offer physical, occupational and other therapies? How often?

Does the organization's dementia special care unit provide a physical environment that is specially designed for the safety of the residents?

6. Your rights as a nursing home resident:

As a resident of a nursing home, you have all the same rights and protections of all United States citizens. In addition, nursing home residents have certain specific rights and protections under the law. Be aware, however, these rights can vary by state. The nursing home must provide you with a written description of your legal rights.

At a minimum, Federal law specifies that a nursing home resident's rights include:
Freedom from Discrimination: Nursing homes do not have to accept all applicants, but they must comply with Civil Rights laws that do not allow discrimination based on race, color, national origin, disability, age or religion under certain conditions.

Respect: You have the right to be treated with dignity and respect. As long as it fits your care plan, you have the right to make your own schedule, including when you go to bed, rise in the morning and eat your meals. You have the right to choose the activities you want to go to.

Freedom from Abuse and Neglect: You have the right to be free from verbal, sexual, physical and mental abuse and involuntary seclusion by anyone. This includes, but is not limited to, nursing home staff, other residents, consultants, volunteers, staff from other agencies, family members or legal guardians, friends or other individuals.

Freedom from Restraints: Physical restraints are any manual method or physical or mechanical device, material or equipment attached to or near your body so you cannot remove the restraint easily. They prevent freedom of movement or normal access to one's own body. A chemical restraint is a drug used to limit freedom of movement and is not needed to treat your medical symptoms. It is against the law for a nursing home to use physical or chemical restraints, unless it is necessary to treat your medical symptoms. Restraints may not be used to punish nor for the convenience of the nursing home staff. You have the right to refuse restraint use unless you are at risk of harming yourself or others.

Information on Services and Fees: You must be informed in writing about services and fees before you move into the nursing home.

The nursing home cannot require a minimum entrance fee as a condition of resistance.

Money: You have the right to manage your own money or to choose someone you trust to do this for you. If you ask the nursing home to manage your personal funds, you must sign a written statement that allows the nursing home to do this for you. However, the nursing home must allow you access to your bank accounts, cash and other financial records. The nursing home must protect your funds from any loss by buying a bond or providing other similar protections. Privacy, Property, and Living Arrangements: You have the right to privacy, and to keep and use your personal belongings and property as long as they do not interfere with the rights, health or safety of others. Nursing home staff should never open your mail unless you allow it. You have the right to use a telephone and talk privately. The nursing home must protect your property from theft. This may include a safe in the facility or cabinets with locked doors in resident rooms. If you and your spouse live in the same nursing home, you are entitled to share a room if you both agree to do so.

Medical Care: You have the right to be informed about your medical condition, medications and to see your own doctor. You also have the right to refuse medications and treatments. You have the right to take part in developing your care plan. You have the right to look at your medical records and reports when you ask.

Visitors: You have the right to spend private time with visitors at any reasonable hour. The nursing home must permit your family to visit you at any time, as long as you wish to see them. You do not have to see any visitor you do not wish to see. Any person who gives you help with your health or legal services may see you at any reasonable time. This includes your doctor, representative from the health department, and your Long-Term Care Ombudsman, among others.

Social Services: The nursing home must provide you with any needed social services, including counseling, help solving problems with other residents, help in contacting legal and financial professionals, and discharge planning.

Leaving the Nursing Home: Living in a nursing home is your choice. You can choose to move to another place. However, the nursing home may have a policy that requires you to tell them before you plan to leave. If you do not, you may have to pay them an extra fee.

If your health allows and your doctor agrees, you can spend time away from the nursing home visiting friends or family during the day or overnight. Talk to the nursing home staff a few days ahead of time if you want to do this so medication and care instructions can be prepared. Caution: If your nursing home care is covered by certain health insurance, you may not be able to leave for visits without losing your coverage.

Complaints: You have the right to make a complaint to the staff of the nursing home, or any other person, without fear of punishment. The nursing home must resolve the issue promptly.

Protection Against Unfair Transfer or Discharge: You cannot be sent to another nursing home, or made to leave the nursing home unless:
• It is necessary for the welfare, health or safety of you or others,
• Your health has declined to the point that the nursing home cannot meet your care needs,
• Your health has improved to the point that nursing home care is no longer necessary,
• The nursing home has not been paid for services you received, or
• The nursing home closes.

Except in emergencies, nursing homes must give a thirty-day written notice of their plan to discharge or transfer you. You have the right to appeal a transfer to another facility. A nursing home cannot make you leave if you are waiting to get Medicaid. The nursing home should work with other state agencies to get payment if a family member or other individual is holding your money.

Your Family and Friends: Family members and legal guardians may meet with the families of other residents and may participate in family councils.

By law, nursing homes must develop a plan of care (care plan) for each resident. You have the right to take part in this process, and family members can help with your care plan with your permission. If your relative is your legal guardian, he or she has the right to look at all medical records about you and has the right to make important decisions on your behalf.

D. Hospice:

1. What do they do?
First, let us clear up a common misperception. Hospice is not a place. It is a type of care. It may be provided in your own home, a hospice facility, a nursing home or some hospitals. Hospice provides end-of-life care, comfort care and/or palliative care. It does not hasten death or postpone death. Instead, it ensures the dying person is as comfortable as possible. Most hospice workers are excellent at pain management and provide the patient with as much dignity as possible.

Hospice workers also help families deal with the impending death of their loved one.

Hospice services usually are provided to patients who are in the last six months of their lives. Often, their illnesses no longer respond to aggressive treatment or the patient and his or her family choose to not undergo aggressive treatment.

2. How do you know if they are good?

Medicare approves certain hospice programs. Not all hospice programs accept Medicare, so not all have gone through the Medicare approval process. The most important factor is to feel comfortable with a particular hospice provider. You need to be confident they will work with you to develop a plan and they will adhere to that plan. Trust your instinct.

3. Who is eligible for Medicare hospice benefits?
Hospice care is covered under Medicare Part A (Hospital

Insurance). You may be eligible for Medicare hospice benefits when you meet all of the following conditions:

• You are eligible for Medicare Part A (Hospital Insurance), and

• Your doctor and the hospice medical director certify you are terminally ill and probably have less than six months to live, and

• You sign a statement choosing hospice care instead of routine Medicare covered benefits for your terminal illness, and

• You receive care from a Medicare-approved hospice program.

Please note that Medicare will often still pay for covered benefits for any health problems that are not related to your terminal illness.

4. Questions to ask:

It often is difficult to broach the topic of hospice. Many people misunderstand and think that hospice is an immediate death sentence. It is not! While it does deal with the end of life, it is a way to live the end of one's life and to define a different approach to medical treatment. It also is not unusual for people to move on and off of hospice care as their conditions change.

The most important thing to remember about hospice is communication is key. Hospice workers are specially trained to help families through this stressful time. You do not need to be embarrassed about anything in front of them. Do not worry if you cannot remember your questions, let alone the answers. That is completely normal. Do not be afraid to ask questions as you remember them, make a list and ask them all at once or ask for clarification if you do not understand. It is vital that the patient and the family know what to expect. For example, while hospice services are available twenty-four hours a day, seven days a week, it does not mean that hospice provides twenty-four hour care to each patient.

Here are some useful questions for you to ask the hospice admissions representative when they visit you:

• Is the hospice licensed, where applicable, and Medicare/Medicaid certified?

- Does the hospice provide the services you want or need? This includes making sure it is religiously and culturally appropriate for you.
- What does hospice expect from you and your caregiver support system? Are you comfortable with this? Is this realistic? Do not feel guilty if you cannot provide the care and support the agency suggests. It is important to be realistic about what you, the family and friends can provide.
- Does the hospice provider adequately support the caregivers?
- Can the hospice provider provide inpatient or respite care if necessary? Where? What are the limitations?
- Are the hospice provider's positions on resuscitation, hydration and antibiotics similar to yours? Make certain you clearly communicate your wishes to them.
- Will your insurance plan work with this hospice provider? How much is covered?
- What out-of-pocket expenses should you anticipate? How much will they cost?
- Is there a sliding scale payment plan for services not covered by insurance?
- Most importantly, are you comfortable with this particular hospice provider? If not, find another.

E. Home care (NOT home HEALTH care) agencies:

We discussed home HEALTH care agencies above. This section addresses home care, often known as companionship services.

These providers primarily deal with the activities of daily living (ADLs)—the things we usually do to take care of ourselves. These include bathing/showering, dressing/undressing, eating/self-feeding, transferring (getting out of bed and into a chair), ambulation (walking), and toileting (or taking care of incontinence).

The providers also support the ADLs through Instrumental Activities of Daily Living (IADLs)—the stuff that makes the ADLs possible. For example, eating is an ADL, but how did the food get onto the plate and in front of the person who is eating it? That process of shopping, cooking and cleaning up is an IADL. IADLs also include things like using the telephone and technology that allow a person to remain independent in their own home.

Home care agencies are excellent resources for providing services for both ADLs and IADLs. They can provide staff to shop, cook, clean, provide companionship and more. Many agencies also have nurses to offer medication management.

Home care agencies often are staffed by certified nursing assistants (CNAs).CNAs undergo specialized training and certification, and if part of an agency, should undergo continuing education and training.

People often make the mistake of assuming anyone can provide these services and hire their next door neighbor's cleaning woman's sister to take care of their mother. Please understand that taking care of an older adult is more than cooking and cleaning. Reputable agencies hire trained professionals, train them, conduct national background checks, are licensed/bonded/insured and have backup plans in place. They are trained to identify and handle emergencies, and they have procedures in place to recognize problems and quickly correct them.

F. Continuing Care Retirement Communities (CCRCs)

"CCRCs are retirement communities that offer more than one kind of housing and different levels of care. In the same community, there may be individual homes or apartments for residents who still live on their own, an assisted living facility for people who need some help with daily care, and a nursing home for those who require more care.

Residents move from one level to another based on their needs, but usually stay within the CCRC. If you are considering a CCRC, be sure to check the nursing home at the CCRC. The nursing home's quality information is on Nursing Home Compare and the nursing home's inspection report should be posted in the nursing home.

Your CCRC contract may require you to use the CCRC's nursing home if you need nursing home care. Some CCRCs will only admit people into their nursing home if they have previously lived in another section of the retirement community, such as their assisted living or independent living.

Many CCRCs require a large payment before you move in (called an entry fee) and charge monthly fees. Find out if a CCRC is accredited and get advice on selecting this type of community from the Commission on Accreditation of Rehabilitation Facilities and the Continuing Care Accreditation Commission (CARF-CCAC) by calling 1-202-587-5001. You also can visit www.carf.org.[12]

The usual model for a CCRC is the resident pays a large up-front fee (often a few hundred thousand dollars)—that may be refundable when the resident leaves the community. This deposit allows the resident to move from independent living to assisted living to a nursing home, if and when needed, while still remaining in the community. Some CCRCs offer a lifetime care commitment—promising not to make the resident leave even if he or she outlives his or her money.

This has created an interesting situation. Many CCRCs are providing such excellent care, their residents are living longer and "living sicker" than originally was planned for. Consequently, there sometimes is a shortage of assisted living or skilled nursing beds within communities. That leaves people in their independent apartments long after they should be. Be sure to ask the question: what happens if my loved one needs to move to assisted living or skilled nursing and the provider is out of beds? If the answer is the provider brings in home health care, ask who is expected to pay for that care. Then, compare that cost to the monthly cost of assisted living in the same CCRC and make sure you are comfortable with the answer.

Questions to ask:

1. How EXACTLY does the down payment/initiation fee/community fee work? How and when is it refundable? Is it adjusted for age and health? Is it adjusted for size of the apartment?

2. What happens if the resident runs out of money? Does the CCRC spend down from the deposit? What happens after the deposit is exhausted? Does the resident have to leave the community?

3. Who provides the medical care on the campus? What happens if the resident needs medical care off campus? Is transportation provided? Is the resident accompanied by CCRC staff? Who pays for what?

4. Is the CCRC financially solvent? With whom is it affiliated?

5. Finally, look at the community in general. Does it seem like a good cultural, social, financial and medical fit?

G. Other places.

Hybrids, group homes, shared housing, co-housing, communes, etcetera. The lines often have become blurred among different types of care providers.

This chapter refers only to the places that claim to be non-institutional or home-like or any other term that implies all large organizations are inherently evil. Quite often, these places try to scare you away from other types of care, or they imply they are the only provider who can help your family member.

Watch anyplace that starts out with a marketing message that refers to "putting" your mother somewhere, institutionalizing her, or anything else that implies it is not her decision to make.

1. What do they say they do?

Many of these places promise the world. They will tell you they assist with medication, but many are not licensed to actually touch the pills. They only can point to the bottle and tell you to take it.

They will tell you they can help with bathing, but they are not licensed to actually touch you. They cannot hold your arm when you get in and out of the tub.

They will tell you they have twenty-four hour staff, but the staff does not necessarily have to be awake. How will your family member let the staff know they need help? What if it is the middle of the night and they cannot get out of bed?

2. What do they usually do?

Many of these places are fine if your family member is well but lonely. They can provide some peace of mind, but PLEASE make sure it is not an artificial peace of mind. Is Mom really safer in a house where all the doors are unlocked and anyone can come in?

Many of these places are not licensed for medical care— and may only offer limited assistance with activities of daily living. So, in some cases, Mom's housemates can be anyone who needs assistance with activities of daily living—not just elderly. Group homes (and other similar organizations) may sometimes house young people and elderly at the same time even if one or the other has severe behavioral problems. This can be a big challenge in a small setting.

So, you really have to look carefully at the care and services provided, not just that the setting seems familiar to you. I do not deny that people, at first glance, would like to live in a house. All I ask is you look to make sure the care is what it needs to be.

What do they do? They will prepare meals, offer activities and do the housekeeping. They will probably have a living room with a television, radio and card table. They may even have a garden. They may let your mom keep her own car.

This may not be a good thing. I heard a story of a woman with the beginning stages of dementia who lived in a group home. She walked out the unlocked door of the house, got into her car and drove away. Fortunately, she did not hit anyone. Unfortunately, she did not know where she was driving to, nor did she know where she lived. Her car was found abandoned in a really rough area of a neighboring city—thirty miles away. Fortunately, the police found her within a few days, unharmed.

I would argue this woman never should have been in this care setting. She needed to be where there is an understanding that she may not recognize danger to herself or others. Someone should have prevented her from leaving the property unescorted, and she never should have had her car and keys so easily accessible. It is not freedom or independence to put this woman in danger.

3. **Things to watch out for.**

I admit I often am afraid of places that are exempted from regulation. A home-like setting is nothing more than a marketing term designed to make you feel more comfortable. Many of the smaller "home-like" organizations are nothing more than a regular house with some modifications. If your family member cannot live alone in his or her own house, what can this particular type of care provide that makes such a big difference?

Having said that, there are some truly caring people who run these small homes. I certainly do not mean to knock their compassion or style, but I strongly urge you to carefully evaluate the medical care your family member will receive and the ability of the care provider to deal with an emergency. Think about it. If there is only one staff person there and a resident needs an ambulance, either the person in the ambulance is alone or the rest of the residents are.

4. **Questions to ask**

Does a qualified staff member conduct a preliminary evaluation of the resident's needs? What are the staff member's qualifications? Can you be involved in this evaluation?

Does the organization create a plan of care for each new resident?

Will you be involved in establishing the plan of care?

Find out who you need to contact or who will contact you when this plan changes.

Does the organization provide the specific services you or your family member need?

The medical side of the equation: The bottom line is... is the medical care the best available?

This is where the JCAHO and Medicare reports come in. The small places may not be inspected, so it may be difficult to compare. If you can compare, how does the facility compare to others? Are you comfortable with their inspection results?

How is the organization staffed during evenings and weekends? How many nurses are on duty? What is the ratio of nurses' aides (CNAs) to residents? Is a physician available at all times?

Is there access to a full-time medical staff of board-certified geriatricians? Consulting specialists? Nurse practitioners?

What routine medical services and facilities are available on-site (for example, x-rays, dental, auditory testing)?

What is the organization's ability to diagnose and treat residents' chronic or acute conditions without transferring to hospitals or other diagnostic facilities?

Does the organization have an affiliation with any medical schools or clinical research programs?

How are medical situations handled if they are beyond the organization's capabilities? If a resident needs to go to the hospital or a specialist, are they accompanied by a staff member from the organization?

Does the organization offer physical, occupational and other therapies? How often?

Does the organization's dementia special care unit provide a physical environment specially designed for the safety of the residents? Again, I go back to the locked door issue. If your mother does not recognize danger to herself or others (a classic definition of dementia), how does she know not to open the door and walk into the street? There is a reason the best facilities have controlled egress.

What precautions are taken for infection control? The larger facilities have strict infection control procedures in place—ask to see the written procedures for this organization. Look to see how trash and dirty laundry are handled.

Food preparation. Depending on the size of this organization, it may not need to have licensed food handlers. What procedures are in place to ensure that your family member does not become ill from a food-borne disease such as salmonella or E. coli? Is there anything to prevent another resident from touching your mother's food? What if they have a cold? Flu? Hepatitis?

Chapter 4

How to choose.

A. Know your options.

Let me say it again. Know your options. Be realistic even when it is tough. It does not do anyone any good if you are looking at retirement communities when your family member really needs assisted living or a nursing home. If you have trouble determining exactly what type of care you need, do not blame yourself—do something about it. Have someone conduct a complete geriatric assessment or talk to your doctor.

Then, expand your horizons. There may not be a place that meets your needs within a fifteen to thirty minute drive of your house. While it is extremely important that you are able to visit your family member on a regular basis, it is more important they live in a place that meets THEIR needs best. Remember, while you may visit two hours every day, they have to live there twenty-four/seven.

B. Become an educated consumer.

Read the inspection reports, surveys and any other available report whenever they are available. Ask for advice from experts when you are unsure of something. Talk to the residents, their families and geriatricians. Be assertive—question things you do not understand or do not make sense to you. This is not the time to be shy.

C. How to look at and evaluate a care provider.

Earlier in this book, we taught you how to read and understand the various inspection reports. Get the reports for the facilities you are interested in and read them. Remember, nothing replaces an on-site visit. So I encourage you to read the reports before you visit the facility and use your best judgment when you visit.

D. What you should expect when you visit (sights, smells, sounds).

Let's be honest. Healthy people do not move into nursing homes. You are going to see frail and ill people. You will see some people who yell, some who cry and some who drool. You will see some people who have tubes in them and some who are missing limbs. On the other hand, you also will see some who look pretty good but may have dementia or something else that is not easy to see. If you drop by very early in the morning, it may not smell as fresh as it will a little later—the staff will change resident's diapers after the residents wake up. However, if you drop by mid- morning or during the afternoon, the organization should smell clean. It should be well-lit, pleasant and cheerful.

Look to see that the residents are up, dressed and interacting with each other and the staff to the best of their ability. The best facilities make sure their residents are as well-groomed as possible. Look for the small things that are very important—is the staff wearing nametags? Do they address the residents by name?

Look for the personality of the place. Some organizations have memory boxes outside the residents' rooms—a great way to get to know the residents better and see what is important to them. Does it feel right to you? Your instincts probably are correct.

Look at the list of activities—is there anything your family member would enjoy doing?

Look at the lounges. What are the residents doing? I have seen some great places where the residents are gathered around a big radio listening to old time programming and enjoying each other's company. I have seen still others where the residents are reading, gardening or simply talking. If all the residents are lined up along the hallway and not in lounges, LEAVE. Be aware some of the newer facilities actually have narrowed their hallways to discourage this behavior and to encourage the use of the lounges. Why? Because there is much more social interaction when the residents are gathered around something instead of staring across at an empty wall.

Talk to the residents. (Be sure to ask permission before you enter anyone's room.)They will be honest with you. I recognize that this may not be practical in a dementia care community.

Try to talk to some people involved with the residents' council or the family council.

If it is a non-profit facility, look at who is on the board or active in the volunteer programs.

Finally, EAT. Yes, I mean eat what the residents eat. You may need to make arrangements for this in advance if you are going to eat in the residents' dining hall. If the marketing info says there is a coffee shop, go there and get a cup of coffee. Cookies and snacks available on a regular basis? Eat them too. Why? Just think about it. Your family member is going to live here. They will have to eat this food seven days a week. It had better be good! Seriously, though. I have been to some organizations where the food is outstanding— even the coffee rivals the best coffee houses. The chefs are creative and the residents are thrilled. Then, I have been to some where the food was so horrible I could not eat it. This just does not make sense to me when we worry about unwanted weight loss in the elderly.

E. Questions you should ask.

The social side of the equation. The bottom line is… will the resident be happy here?

This is where you come in. These questions are more qualitative than quantitative. Only you and your family member can decide whether this is a good fit.

Is the community involved in the organization?

Does the organization have volunteers who work in the resident care areas? What do they do? Are you comfortable with this?

Are you and the resident comfortable with the organization's resident rights and responsibilities information? You should be provided this information in writing.

Is attention given to individual food preferences? Is the food

nutritionally and culturally appropriate?

Can substitutions be made to the menu? Can food be brought in

from the outside?

Are the resident's individual psychosocial needs attended to? Is the

environment comforting?

Are there diverse and interesting activity programs?

Are there opportunities to attend appropriate religious services?
How often?

Is there a garden?

Is there a well-stocked gift shop?

Is there a beauty salon? Barber shop? Manicurist available? Does

the organization have an appealing ambiance?

Does the organization allow/encourage pets?

What is the organization's philosophy about end-of-life decisions?
Does this philosophy match your beliefs? If not, will the organization
agree to abide by the resident's decision? Make sure you are clear
on exactly what the organization will or will not do— some
organizations, for example, will not remove a feeding tube once it
has been placed.

E. Answers you should expect.

First, bear in mind this is the residents' home. Yes, people are here
for health care, but this still is their home. Within reason, an
organization should do everything in its power to make your family
member comfortable.

So, expect to feel welcome. Expect to be treated with respect and
dignity and expect the same for your family member.

Expect to have your questions answered honestly. If you feel someone is trying to sell you a bill of goods—leave.

Expect there to be trained staff members to help your family member make this transition.

Expect to see kind, caring staff members. If you do not—leave.

It is really important to understand there are phenomenal eldercare options out there. The best are innovative and at the forefront of geriatric medicine. They also clearly demonstrate true understanding and compassion for their residents. I guarantee it will be obvious to you if you are in such a facility.

G. Helpful tips.

Looking at multiple organizations can be even more confusing than looking to buy a new house or choosing a college. So, here are some helpful hints. I apologize if they seem obvious, but it never hurts to include them.

1. Do not visit more than three or four facilities in one day. You will not be able to really explore the organizations, and they will all blend together.

2. Bring a camera, notepad, pen and a list of questions. Be sure to make notes of which pictures go with which facility.

3. Be sure to pick up the organization's marketing material, resident newsletters, family newsletters, menu for the month, etcetera.

4. Make notes about things you especially like or dislike.

5. Again, ask questions. If you have a special concern, raise it. Do not be afraid or intimidated. You are the customer.

6. Open the door for the staff to tell you what they like and dislike about the organization. Be aware, however, some staff are completely opposed to residential care communities and think people always should live at home. I am still not sure why people like this would take a job at a facility, but sometimes they do.

7.   Finally, once again, trust yourself. At this point in the process, you know your family member needs more medical care and support than he or she can get on his or her own. You have understood that some sort of care option is necessary. So, once you have narrowed the list down to places that can provide the best care and your family member will be comfortable in, go with your gut instinct. You will know what the best fit is.

H.   What makes this provider different than all other providers?

How to look beyond the basics:
Many places have something special about them. These are the true stories that make me glad to have been a part of the eldercare industry. Look around when you are visiting. If you are in a good place, you will probably see something special.

1.   Once there was an egg. There is an outstanding nursing home that was led by one of the most compassionate people I've ever met. His nursing home was so well-run, his own mother lived in it. On one of his regular walks around the home, he stopped to chat with a long-time resident. When he asked her if there was anything he could do to make her happier or more comfortable, she smiled and said she'd really like an egg over easy. Turns out she hadn't had one in over fifteen years—since she'd come to the home. Why? Nursing home populations are susceptible to food-borne diseases and almost all breakfast-type egg items are made from the pasteurized eggs that come in cartons. So, everything is scrambled, made into omelets or quiche. Also, it's really hard to cook individual eggs for so many people. None of this was a good reason or excuse for the CEO and his head chef. So, they figured out a way to make eggs to order once a month or so, made sure the eggs were cooked to the proper temperature, and safe. Yes, it took a lot of effort, and some of the staff was really unhappy about the extra workload, but in the end, everyone appreciated it, and the residents were thrilled.

2.   The shower. Many Holocaust survivors are terrified of using tile-lined showers in the bathrooms. It reminds them too much of the gas chambers. Many organizations that serve this population have entirely changed the designs of the bathrooms so they are not

scary. They're larger, brighter and more expensive than standard stalls, but it really makes the residents more comfortable.

3. The chef. I met a head chef from a large multi-service campus. This is a man who is a great cook. He knows that most of the women who live on the campus used to entertain and prepare family meals. He also understands how important that is to them. I've heard from some of the residents that he will sit down with them, discuss their recipes and prepare small batches of their dishes when their families come to visit. He then delivers them to their apartments where they can heat the meals up in their kitchenettes. He allows them the dignity of cooking for their families.

4. Using the wisdom of old age. There is a beautiful retirement community with an oceanfront view. Truly luxurious. The next town over, however, is comprised mostly of newly arrived immigrants who do not speak English, and is primarily low-income. The administration of the retirement community partnered with one of the schools in the next town, got a grant for computers and Internet access, and created a pen-pal program. The students came to the retirement community, taught the seniors how to use the computers, and in return, the seniors teach the students English. In addition to regular visits, they e-mail each other all the time and have had many parties together.

5. The laundry room. I once visited a new nursing home in the Midwest. I was on a tour when we arrived on a floor that was so brightly lit, it took me a minute to get used to it. Then, I passed an open lounge area that had a washer and dryer and a big table full of different sized towels dumped on it—all different colors and sizes and materials, but all square. They were next to an empty laundry basket. This seemed really strange to me since there was a huge laundry room in the basement and a staff that took care of all linens and clothes. Much to my surprise, a resident walked by, looked at the laundry, folded it all and put it into the basket. As soon as she walked away, the staff person I was with dumped the laundry back out of the basket and onto the table. By now, my puzzlement must have been obvious, because the staff member finally 'fessed up'. We were on the dementia floor. The brighter, ambient light makes the residents less agitated, and the activity of folding laundry stimulates their minds using different textures, etcetera, in an

activity they still remember. The washer and dryer? Fakes. I admit I was skeptical, but when I spoke to the residents on the floor about their day and activities, they told me they had done the laundry. I was amazed so many of these residents could discuss the laundry with me. They talked about colors. Then, they talked about how they used to do laundry without the help of the fancy machines. Really, they got a lot of pleasure out of it!

6.   Shoes. In my opinion, the volunteers who work in long-term care facilities are incredible. While I have become somewhat used to their caring and compassion, I admit that they sometimes still surprise me. Here's one case. There was a nursing home that had some very frail, very destitute residents. One day, a volunteer noticed one of the residents was wearing very well-worn shoes. This resident had no family—she had outlived them all—and very little money. So, this volunteer got together with some of the other volunteers, they pooled their own money, and took off for the mall's big summer sale. They returned to the nursing home with cars full of shoes and went floor to floor giving the residents new shoes. Pretty ones. Not all good-for-you shoes have to be unattractive, you know. The best part was they never made the residents feel as though they were accepting charity. Instead, they told the truth to the residents—the sale at the mall was just too good to pass up.

Chapter 5

How to pay for it all:

Paying for care is so complicated that it is a book unto itself. I will attempt a basic explanation here.

First, I cannot emphasize enough—go to a financial advisor and make a plan while you are young enough to do so. Your attorney and/or accountant should be able to recommend one. Make sure the professional you choose is licensed and comes highly recommended. Watch out for sharks and cheats.

Second, make sure you have debunked myths. Medicare is NOT going to pay for everything you or your family needs. Medicaid is not going to either, unless you are legitimately destitute, have a true medical need (as defined by Medicaid) and are living full-time in a nursing home or are a participant in a Medicaid waiver program.

Third, make sure not to create your financial plan in a vacuum. You need to consider health, family support, longevity and the real cost of care that is appropriate for your family member. I cannot tell you how many times I have seen financial planners and attorneys tie up money to protect it from Medicaid and to preserve it for the children or grandchildren, then leave the older adult in a position where they cannot pay for home care or assisted living when they need it.

Also—do NOT just add your name onto bank accounts or investment accounts with your parent. It can affect your and their eligibility for benefits.

Some tools for payment:

Long Term Care insurance (LTC Insurance). This can be an important planning tool and pay for care when you need it. The best plans cover home care, home health care, assisted living and nursing homes. When choosing, be sure you find a reputable company that is financially stable, has a long history in the business and is not likely to go bankrupt. Also, make sure you compare the daily benefit amount as it compares to the actual cost of care. While

$200 a day benefit may seem like a lot, if your care costs $500 per day, you still need to come up with $300 per day out of pocket. So, think about what type of care you would like, see what it costs today, and plan accordingly.

It is really important for you to understand how the plan can be cancelled, how to trigger the policy if you need to go on claim and how the inflation factor works.

It also is important to choose the appropriate term for the policy. Three years? Five years? Lifetime? Know the caps, and again, make this decision based on your lifestyle, family medical history, family support etcetera.

This is not the time to be shy. Compare and contrast plans and providers.

I would recommend reviewing the information on the American Association for Long Term Care Insurance's website http://www.aaltci.org.

Veteran's Aid and Attendance. This is a little-known benefit for veterans and their surviving spouses who require the regular attendance of another person to assist in eating, bathing, dressing/undressing or toileting—as verified by your doctor. This benefit, as of 2011, can provide up to $1,632 per month to a veteran, $1,055 per month to a surviving spouse, or $1,949 per month to a couple.[13]

There is an amazing website—http://www.veteranaid.org that has links to all the forms you will need, explanations, guides you through what to expect and more. It is amazing!

Chapter 6

The doctor did not specifically say I could not fly an airplane... Walking the fine line between preserving independence and protecting your family and friends.

No, I am not making this up. I heard of a man who had undergone chemotherapy and radiation. The doctors told him he should not operate heavy machinery while he was undergoing this particular phase of treatment. No one is sure if he was agitated because of the treatments, bored, or just being obstinate, but he was going to fly his plane. He demanded to know where it said he could not fly his plane. He was correct that the notes from his doctor did not specifically say that he could not fly a plane. Everyone else, however, assumed airplanes were under the category of heavy machinery. They were able to strike a compromise—his daughter drove him to the airport where he and a mechanic went over the plane to make sure everything was okay, but he did not fly it. We think the only reason this worked was because the airports were on a heightened security alert and the small planes were surrounded by armed National Guardsmen.

Flying an airplane may be an extreme example, but we have all seen the issue about driving. Taking away a driver's license creates a whole host of social problems from writing checks to being a passenger on an airplane. It also represents a huge loss of independence. So, even though many states have non-driver identification cards, it still presents an issue. Also, we all know taking away a license does not stop a determined senior citizen from driving. One family, truly desperate to stop the grandfather from driving, tried everything. They had the doctor talk to him, the Department of Motor Vehicles failed him on his driver's test, his license was taken away and still he drove—on the sidewalk, into parked cars, etcetera. This man was a real danger to himself and others. The family took away his car keys, and he called a locksmith to get more. Finally, the granddaughter asked if she could borrow the car to go to the mall. He gave her the keys, and off she went. A few hours later, she called him crying because the car had been "stolen."He was not upset, he was just glad she was okay. The car was "stolen" by another family member who parked it in long-term parking at the airport. They were afraid he would spot the car if they parked it at one of their houses. The family figured if he got used to not having the car, they could break him of his reckless driving. It worked. I am not sure I would recommend this solution, but desperate times called for creative measures.

The tailor, the craftsman, the artist and the gardener.
A resident of a nursing home in Boston had been a tailor for years before he got too ill to take care of himself. In Maryland, a man had been a woodworker/sculptor and an artist. In Virginia, a woman had been a gardener. All these people were fortunate to move into facilities that recognized and respected their talents and had the resources to do something about it. So, the tailor was given some space to sew in, the woodworker and his buddies got a woodshop (and supervision), the artist got some painting space and the gardener got a raised flowerbed and some indoor space with great lighting. Preserving independence can be as simple as making safety adjustments and adding supervision, BUT this does not apply to things that are truly dangerous.

Do not wait for the car accident, the house fire or the fall down the stairs before addressing the safety issue.

Chapter 7

Now that you have found care, what comes next?

A. Home Health Care and Home Care: 1. Things to expect.

Expect a kind, caring, well-trained professional to help your family member. Do not accept anything less. If you have asked the questions listed in the chapter on home health care, you should have a reasonable idea of what services can/will be provided.

Also, however, expect an adjustment period. Your family member may not be used to having a stranger in the house let alone one who is performing intimate tasks. Keep your eyes and ears open, but do not rush to judgment unless you think your family member is in immediate danger. In that case, dial 911.

2. Things to watch out for

a.   Deterioration of health. If you see signs of deterioration in any of those categories, call the doctor and insist on bringing your family member in for a visit.

b.   Elder abuse or neglect. This is discussed in detail in the appendix. Some quick advice before you read on…If for even one second you think someone's life or health is in immediate jeopardy, call 911. Do not hesitate. There is no penalty if you are wrong, but there is a big problem if you are right and do not do anything about it.

c.   Theft. First, I hope you took some precautions and removed the valuables from the house before the caregiver came in. Second, I urge you to make sure the item(s) really were stolen and not misplaced. Most home health aides are licensed, bonded and honest. However, if there really is a problem, call the head of the home health agency right away. If that does not work, call the police at the non-emergency number. They will help.

d.   Depression/suicide. This is also discussed in detail in the appendix. If something strikes you as wrong, address it immediately. It may be a side effect of a medication, but you need a trained professional to make that judgment. If you think someone is suicidal and may be prepared to act on it, dial 911.

e.   Dementia. At the beginning of the book, we discussed the warning signs of Alzheimer's/dementia. Remember that some medicines and depression can mimic these signs. When in doubt, see the doctor and make sure the proper tests are done.

3. Things to make your life easier

Meal preparation:
I remember standing in the kitchen with my parents as we made TV dinners for my elderly grandfather. He was not able to cook on his own, and this was before microwaves were invented. So, we created an assembly line with food from the Kosher caterer and put together compete meals in little aluminum foil containers. All he had to do was reheat them in the toaster oven. Despite our best efforts to create balanced meals and watch his sodium content, he would eat all the corned beef and leave all of the chicken.

Times have changed, but the concept has not. My friends and I all are pressed for time and often do not cook good meals for ourselves. So, we have tried something new and it works great for feeding our elderly relatives too. First, go to one of those big warehouse stores, and buy a few big packages of meat (some of the prepared stuff you cook yourself is really good), a big thing of rice, potatoes or other starch, and either frozen vegetables or relatively indestructible ones that can be frozen. Then, buy all the comfort food you can find. Then, go to the dollar store and invest in lots of the plastic round divided containers with lids. They are about two inches deep. I am being specific about the containers because I have gone through much trial and error. The less expensive, disposable kind have lids that shatter when they are dropped out of the freezer—a common occurrence if the senior has balance issues. The other kinds of containers tend to leave the food mixed in a clump and are hard to reheat in the microwave. These plate-like ones not only survive the drop-on-the-floor test, but also have high enough edges that people can eat right out of the container, even if they have mobility issues.

Okay. So, now you have food and containers. Go home and cook. Cook the things you and your elderly relatives like to eat. Cook lots of it. You are going to want to stock up. If you hate to cook, buy the prepared stuff and divide it into single portion servings. Divide up the comfort food into easy to manage portions. I am a big fan of the multi-packs of single-serve cookies, crackers and nuts. The bigger ones always seem to go stale before I finish them.

Why are you doing this? Because you are going to assemble tasty, easy to microwave dinners. Then, you are going to stock your freezer and your family member's freezer and pantry. This means if you or they cannot get out to do grocery shopping, it will not be a crisis. It also means you know they have the opportunity to eat well. Anything you make will have less sodium than most of the frozen dinners we are all tempted to buy. Besides, I am sure your food tastes better. Finally, it buys you some time. We have all had those days when we are so tired we eat dry cereal (the milk went bad and we did not have time to get more), crackers, or ice cream for dinner. When you have an elderly relative who needs help, your time becomes even more valuable. So, save it where you can.

Shopping:
My friend is kept running constantly by her parents' needing stuff at stores. Some of it is really necessary. The rest of it probably could wait a few hours without becoming a crisis. Save yourself time. Have backups of the things they use on a regular basis and make sure your parents know where they are. Toothpaste, toilet paper, aspirin, and many other items last a long time. If they always have a spare, you will be less likely to get a call at 10:00 at night that they have run out of toothpaste.

Also, many supermarkets deliver for a small fee. You can order online and schedule the delivery. Look into this—they will even remember what you ordered last time.

Finally, an emergency box.
We all have seen Federal Emergency Management Agency's (FEMA) recommendations for keeping an emergency box. I admit, I tried to make one like they said, and I could not lift it. So, I have come up with a few suggestions of my own. Buy all these things and put them into a plastic box with a lid and handles. It will be

sturdy, easy to lift and will not break if it gets wet. Then, put the box somewhere easy to reach, even if the power has gone out. I am operating under the assumption that unless it is a dire emergency that involves evacuation, the senior will need to be able to stay put in the house for a few days without electricity.

Flashlights with the batteries in them. It is tough to start putting batteries in the flashlights when the power has already gone out. I am partial to the flashlights that have a wide base and can stand up on their own and serve as a beacon or lantern. Buy lots. Ideally, if the power goes out, there should be enough flashlights to keep the house well-lit (prevents falls).

Extra batteries for the flashlights. Again, be sure to open the plastic. I was very surprised to find out the rechargeable flashlights did not last as long as the regular ones. With the power out, the ridiculous thing would not charge!

Be careful about candles. I have heard one too many stories of fires caused by candles. If you insist on using them, at least get the ones in the jar.

A first aid kit you have already removed the plastic from.

A few small bottles of water. You should keep a bigger supply of bottled water elsewhere in the house.

A box of protein bars, granola bars, etcetera with a long shelf life.

A list of all important phone numbers written in large enough print to be seen in low light.

Other things to have in case of emergency (that do not need to be in the box).

A phone that works even when the power goes out. I still have my old princess phone landline from childhood. It was the only thing that worked when the power went out.

A radio or television that operates on batteries.

Enough bottled water for three days. Smaller bottles usually are easier to handle than the gallon-sized ones.

Food with a long shelf life that can be eaten cold. Also, if you buy canned food, make sure there is a manual can opener and that the senior can handle it. Otherwise, buy the tuna in envelopes instead of cans and buy the canned foods that have pull-off tops.

A second list of emergency phone numbers posted someplace obvious.

4. Do not forget the manicures…

Things to make your family member's life easier and more enjoyable.

Ask before you come over. Maybe your family member is tired and wants to be left alone.

Include your family member in family events whenever possible. I do not just mean Thanksgiving and other major holidays, I mean school plays, soccer games, movies, dinners out—whatever the elder can physically handle.

Set up regular flower deliveries.

Bring books. There is a special program through the Library of Congress that provides electronic readers for people who are legally blind.

Buy a computer with Internet access. Older adults CAN use them— you just may need to make the typeface on the screen larger.

Buy or record movies and bring them over.

Finally, do not forget the manicures. If your relative is house-bound, see if a local manicurist can come by to file her nails and do a polish change. The licensing requirements vary state by state, but there are some that will allow this.

5. What to do if there is a problem

First, determine if this is a situation that immediately threatens anyone's life or health. If it is, dial 911.If not, ask pointed questions of both the elder and the caregiver (ask them separately while the other is not in the room).

a.   Theft: Keep in mind that questions of theft can just as easily be items being misplaced. If you really think items may have been stolen, ask the caregiver if he or she has seen them. Do not accuse anyone of theft unless you are sure. If you are, call the owner of the Home Health Agency immediately. Discuss the situation with them first. Just a reminder, you should remove valuables from the house or lock them away before you have any type of caregiver come in.

b.   Physical harm. If you suspect elder abuse (see warning signs in the appendix), call the police. Then, let them guide you through dealing with the owner of the agency.

c.   Once you have taken care of the immediate problem, you may want to report it to the Eldercare Ombudsman's Office for your state.

B. Residential Care:

1.   Get a list of people who work in the Residential Care facilities you have chosen along with their job descriptions. This should include who to call with specific questions and their contact information. Make sure your private doctor and the facility doctors have each other's contact information, too.

Make sure you speak to the admissions staff and the rest of your loved one's team to learn how to participate in care plan meetings and family council meetings.

2.   Become familiar with the usual facility routines—meals, activities, emergency procedures, when people are transported to the hospital, visiting hours, taking the person out of the facility for visits, overnight stays, etcetera.

3.   Understand there is a transition period, similar to when kids first go off to camp or college. The older adult may be sad, unhappy or angry. This is part of the normal transition and usually gets better after a few weeks.

4. Exceptions to #3 above: Things to watch out for. We wish these never would happen but sometimes do.

a.   Signs of elder abuse or neglect. Detailed signs of abuse and neglect are in the appendix. Just remember—if you suspect someone is being physically abused and is in danger, dial 911 immediately. Let the trained professionals make the judgment. Nothing bad will happen to you if it turns out the senior really did fall by accident. Think about it, though—what if you were right to suspect abuse and did not call?

Also, you should feel free to use the services of your state's eldercare ombudsman. They will be happy to help you file any necessary complaints.

b.   Signs of depression/suicidal behavior. What to do. Most residential care facilities that provide any sort of medical services will notice if a resident is becoming depressed. Those that are certified by Medicare actually MUST review a resident's mental health. However, you may notice something before anyone else does. First, bring it to the attention of the medical staff. Then, ask what specifically they will do to look into this, when it will be done and what you can expect next. If you do not like the answer, get mad! Move up the chain of command until you get the answers you need. Do not hesitate to bring your elder's doctor into it.

c.   Theft. What to do. Keep in mind that questions of theft can just as easily be items being misplaced. If you really think items may have been stolen, ask the staff if they have seen them. Do not accuse anyone of theft unless you are sure. Sometimes, residents may borrow things from each other, or they may not know they have taken something that is not theirs. If you are sure a valuable was stolen, call the CEO or Administrator of the agency immediately.

d.   Signs of increasing dementia in a patient who was NOT diagnosed with dementia. This can be a warning sign of depression or adverse reaction to medication and needs to be addressed immediately. Bring it to the attention of the medical staff and/or your elder's own physician.

Things to make your life easier.

If your family member is in a residential care organization, she probably has most of her meals taken care of. However, homemade treats are always welcome. If your family member does not have a refrigerator in his/her room, ask the staff if you can keep a small snack elsewhere. Be sure to check with the staff about what they recommend. You do not want to store food where it will attract bugs.

Ask the staff for their suggestions regarding purchasing clothing, socks, bathrobes and other items. You will be surprised at the depth of their ideas, and stocking up on these items and keeping them at your house will prevent you from running around at the last minute looking for them. By the way, you may need to label the clothing – just like you do for camp.

Don't forget the manicures…

Things to make your family member's life easier and more enjoyable.

Ask before you come over. Maybe your family member is tired and wants to be left alone. If you say you will visit, be sure and do so at the time you said you will be there.

Include your family member in family events whenever possible. I do not just mean Thanksgiving and other major holidays, I mean school plays, soccer games, movies, dinners out—whatever the elder can physically handle.

Set up regular flower deliveries.

Bring books.

Buy or record movies and bring them over. There are some small DVD players these days. Check with the facility to see if they are allowed.

Finally, do not forget the manicures. If your relative is house-bound, see if a local manicurist can come by to file her nails and do a polish change. The licensing requirements vary state by state, but there are some that will allow this.

What to do if there is a problem.

Before we begin:
Recognize the difference between a real problem and an annoyance. The signs of elder abuse are detailed in the appendix. Any of those signs are a real problem. Missing nightgowns, soap and slippers are an annoyance—and entirely common in dementia units. Not liking the food needs to be addressed. Most of the better facilities will notice if one of their residents is not eating, so be sure to ask the staff about this issue.

Also, keep in mind that perceptions of time vary. I have stood in residents' rooms in nursing homes with the CEOs and pushed the emergency response buttons. We have timed the response. It is amazing how long forty-five seconds feels like when you are waiting. So, if your family member complains that no one responds to the call buttons, try it yourself. If it is a perception, great. If it is a real problem, you need to address it.

So, now that you have established there is a real problem.

First, do not hesitate. If you think something is seriously wrong, look into it. I am not saying you need to call the CEO of the facility or the police because a pair of socks is missing, but your family member deserves the best care possible. The best care providers have grievance procedures in place.

If the official procedures do not work, go directly to the CEO or the administrator. The good ones will listen to you and address your concerns. Remember, you are not bothering them. It is their job to oversee the organization. Quite frankly, most of them would rather find out about a problem before it becomes life-threatening.

If the CEO/administrator route does not work, call your state's eldercare ombudsman. They will help walk you through the next steps.

Second, let me repeat. Do not hesitate. If you think something/someone is jeopardizing your family member's health, GET HELP. If it is an immediate threat, call 911.

Appendix

Warning signs of elder abuse and what to do about it.

The National Center on Elder Abuse has developed some very specific definitions of elder abuse. They are listed below. Before you read this list, let me again remind you…If you think someone may possibly be a victim of elder abuse, contact your police or local social service agency. If it is or could be a life threatening emergency, dial 911.

Physical Abuse

Physical abuse is defined as the use of physical force that may result in bodily injury, physical pain, or impairment. Physical abuse may include but is not limited to such acts of violence as striking (with or without an object), hitting, beating, pushing, shoving, shaking, slapping, kicking, pinching and burning. In addition, inappropriate use of drugs and physical restraints, force-feeding and physical punishment of any kind also are examples of physical abuse.

Signs and symptoms of physical abuse include but are not limited to:
- *bruises, black eyes, welts, lacerations, and rope marks,*
- *bone fractures, broken bones, and skull fractures,*
- *open wounds, cuts, punctures, untreated injuries in various stages of healing,*
- *sprains, dislocations, and internal injuries/bleeding,*
- *broken eyeglasses/frames, physical signs of being subjected to punishment, and signs of being restrained,*
- *laboratory findings of medication overdose or underutilization of prescribed drugs,*
- *an elder's report of being hit, slapped, kicked, or mistreated,*
- *an elder's sudden change in behavior; and*
- *the caregiver's refusal to allow visitors to see an elder alone.*

Sexual Abuse

Sexual abuse is defined as non-consensual sexual contact of any kind with an elderly person. Sexual contact with any person incapable of giving consent is also considered sexual abuse. It includes, but is not limited to, unwanted touching, all types of sexual assault or battery, such as rape, sodomy, coerced nudity and sexually explicit photographing.

Signs and symptoms of sexual abuse include but are not limited to:
- *bruises around the breasts or genital area,*
- *unexplained venereal disease or genital infections,*
- *unexplained vaginal or anal bleeding,*
- *torn, stained, or bloody underclothing; and*
- *an elder's report of being sexually assaulted or raped.*

Emotional or Psychological Abuse

Emotional or psychological abuse is defined as the infliction of anguish, pain or distress through verbal or nonverbal acts. Emotional/psychological abuse includes but is not limited to verbal assaults, insults, threats, intimidation, humiliation and harassment. In addition, treating an older person like an infant, isolating an elderly person from his or her family, friends or regular activities, giving an older person the silent treatment and enforced social isolation are examples of emotional/psychological abuse.

Signs and symptoms of emotional/psychological abuse include but are not limited to:
- *being emotionally upset or agitated,*
- *being extremely withdrawn and non-communicative or non-responsive,*
- *unusual behavior usually attributed to dementia (for example, sucking, biting, rocking) and*
- *an elder's report of being verbally or emotionally mistreated.*

Neglect

Neglect is defined as the refusal or failure to fulfill any part of a person's obligations or duties to an elder. Neglect may also include failure of a person who has fiduciary responsibilities to provide care for an elder (for example, pay for necessary home care services) or the failure on the part of an in-home service provider to provide necessary care.

Neglect typically means the refusal or failure to provide an elderly person with such life necessities as food, water, clothing, shelter, personal hygiene, medicine, comfort, personal safety and other essentials included in an implied or agreed-upon responsibility to an elder.

Signs and symptoms of neglect include but are not limited to:
- *dehydration, malnutrition, untreated bed sores and poor personal hygiene,*
- *unattended or untreated health problems,*
- *hazardous or unsafe living condition/arrangements (such as improper wiring, no heat or no running water),*
- *unsanitary and unclean living conditions (such as dirt, fleas, lice on person, soiled bedding, fecal/urine smell, inadequate clothing) and*
- *an elder's report of being mistreated.*

Abandonment

Abandonment is defined as the desertion of an elderly person by an individual who has assumed responsibility for providing care for an elder, or by a person with physical custody of an elder.

Signs and symptoms of abandonment include but are not limited to:
- *the desertion of an elder at a hospital, nursing facility or other similar institution,*
- *the desertion of an elder at a shopping center or other public location, and*
- *an elder's own report of being abandoned.*

Financial or Material Exploitation

Financial or material exploitation is defined as the illegal or improper use of an elder's funds, property or assets. Examples include, but are not limited to, cashing an elderly person's checks without authorization or permission, forging an older person's signature, misusing or stealing an older person's money or possessions, coercing or deceiving an older person into signing any document (for example, contracts or a will), and the improper use of conservatorship, guardianship or power of attorney.

Signs and symptoms of financial or material exploitation include but are not limited to:
- *sudden changes in bank account or banking practice, including an unexplained withdrawal of large sums of money by a person accompanying the elder,*
- *the inclusion of additional names on an elder's bank signature card,*
- *unauthorized withdrawal of the elder's funds using the elder's ATM card,*
- *abrupt changes in a will or other financial documents,*
- *unexplained disappearance of funds or valuable possessions,*
- *substandard care being provided or bills unpaid despite the availability of adequate financial resources,*
- *discovery of an elder's signature being forged for financial transactions or for the titles of his/her possessions,*
- *sudden appearance of previously uninvolved relatives claiming their rights to an elder's affairs and possessions,*
- *unexplained sudden transfer of assets to a family member or someone outside the family,*
- *the provision of services that are not necessary, and*
- *an elder's report of financial exploitation.*

Self-neglect

Self-neglect is characterized as the behavior of an elderly person that threatens his or her own health or safety. Self-neglect generally manifests itself in an older person as a refusal or failure to provide him or herself with adequate food, water, clothing, shelter, personal hygiene, medication (when indicated) and safety precautions.

The definition of self-neglect excludes a situation in which a mentally competent older person, who understands the consequences of his or her decisions, makes a conscious and voluntary decision to engage in acts that threaten his or her health or safety as a matter of personal choice.

119

Signs and symptoms of self-neglect include but are not limited to:
- *dehydration, malnutrition, untreated or improperly attended medical conditions and poor personal hygiene,*
- *hazardous or unsafe living conditions/arrangements (such as improper wiring, no indoor plumbing, no heat, no running water),*
- *unsanitary or unclean living quarters (for example, animal/insect infestation, no functioning toilet, fecal/urine smell),*
- *inappropriate and/or inadequate clothing, lack of necessary medical aids (such as eyeglasses, hearing aids, dentures), and*
- *grossly inadequate housing or homelessness.*

Signs of depression in the elderly

Depression is a medical illness characterized by persistent sadness, discouragement and loss of self-worth. These feelings are often accompanied by reduced energy and concentration, sleep problems (insomnia), decreased appetite and/or weight loss. In the elderly, it also frequently presents with excessive concerns about bodily aches and pains.

Causes, incidence, and risk factors

Detecting depression in the elderly may be complicated by several factors. Often the symptoms of depression such as fatigue, loss of appetite and sleeping difficulties are associated with the aging process or a medical condition rather than with major depressive disorder.

Contributing factors include the loss of a spouse or close friends, chronic pain and illness, difficulty with mobility, frustration with memory loss, difficulty adapting to changing circumstances such as moving from a home to a retirement facility, or changes within the family.

Depression can also be a sign of a medical problem. It may be complicated by brain disorders associated with the aging process such as Alzheimer's disease.

Depression in the elderly is a widespread problem that is often not diagnosed and frequently undertreated. Many older individuals will not admit to signs and symptoms of depression for fear of being seen as weak or crazy.

Symptoms
- depressed or irritable mood
- feelings of worthlessness or sadness
- loss of interest or pleasure in daily activities
- temper, agitation
- change in appetite, usually a loss of appetite
- change in weight
- unintentional weight loss (most frequent)
- weight gain
- difficulty sleeping
- daytime sleepiness
- difficulty falling asleep (initial insomnia)
- multiple awakenings through the night (middle insomnia)
- early morning awakening (terminal insomnia)
- fatigue (tiredness or weariness)
- difficulty concentrating
- memory loss
- abnormal thoughts, excessive or inappropriate guilt
- excessively irresponsible behavior pattern
- abnormal thoughts about death
- thoughts about suicide
- plans to commit suicide or actual suicide attempts

If these symptoms are present every day for more than 2 weeks, then depression is likely present.

Signs and tests
- a physical examination will help determine if there is a medical illness causing the depression
- psychological evaluation
- blood tests: CBC or blood differential, thyroid function tests, liver or kidney function tests
- a variety of other tests may be indicated

Treatment

Sometimes depression can be alleviated by social interventions to help with isolation or loneliness such as group outings, volunteer work for the healthy elderly or regular visits from concerned people. Treatment of underlying medical conditions or the discontinuation of certain medications may alleviate symptoms.

Antidepressant drug therapy has been shown to increase quality of life in depressed elderly patients. These medications are carefully monitored for side effects and doses are usually lower and increased more slowly than in younger adults.

Neuroleptic medications may help treat agitation in some individuals. Electroconvulsive therapy (ECT) may be indicated in the severely depressed if other measures are unsuccessful.

Expectations (prognosis)

If detected, depression may respond to medical treatment. Undetected, it may lead to complications. The outcome is usually worse for those who have limited access to social services, or to family or friends who can help promote an interest in activities.

Complications

Depression may be complicated by Alzheimer's disease or other forms of dementia. It may also complicate other medical conditions in the elderly. Untreated depression in the elderly is associated with a high rate of suicide.

Calling your health care provider

Call your health care provider if you are feeling worthless or hopeless or if you are crying frequently.

Also call if you feel you are having difficulty coping with stresses in your life and want a referral for counseling.

Go to the nearest emergency room or call your local emergency number (such as 911) if you are having thoughts of suicide or of taking your own life.

If you are caring for an aging family member and think they might *be suffering from depression, contact their health care provider.*

Often, older patients will not admit to signs and symptoms of depression out of pride".[14]

About the Author

Jodi L. Lyons

With more than twenty years' experience in the nonprofit healthcare arena, Jodi has been a leader in organizations representing healthcare and long-term care service providers. A graduate of Brandeis University, Jodi is on the Board of the Alzheimer's Association, National Capital Area, and is the founder of Senior Sherpa, the tailor-made guide to managing healthcare, custodial care, financial and legal needs for aging adults -- offering customized in-person and online resources available around the clock.

For more information:
Twitter: @jodilyons1 www.myelderresources.com
http://blog.myelderresources.com/
www.senior-sherpa.com

Find more books from Keith Publications, LLC At
www.keithpublications.com

Endnotes

[1] www.strokeassociation.org

[2] http://www.nhlbi.nih.gov/actintime/

[3] Copyright 2004 Alzheimer's Association www.alz.org

[4] Copyright 2004 Alzheimer's Association www.alz.org

[5] Copyright 2004 Alzheimer's Association www.alz.org

[6] 'Lectric Law Library. www.lectlaw.com

[7] http://www.lotsahelpinghands.com/

[8] http://www.jointcommission.org/facts_about_the_joint_commission/

[9] US General Accounting Office publication GAO-04-684 – assisted living. page 4

[10] US General Accounting Office publication GAO-04-684 – assisted living. page 7

[11] Joint Commission on Accreditation of Healthcare Organizations, www.jcaho.org, One Renaissance Blvd. Oakbrook Terrace, IL 60181

[12] http://www.medicare.gov/NHCompare/Static/tabSI.asp?language=English&acti veTab=3&subTab=3&Alternatives=HCAHPS8

[13] www.veteranaid.org

[14] Medline Plus – a service of the National Library of Medicine and the National Institutes of Health. http://www.nlm.nih.gov/medlineplus/ency

CPSIA information can be obtained at www.ICGtesting.com
Printed in the USA
LVOW06s1800060514

384656LV00027B/1316/P